GREEK VASES

Dyfri Williams

Published for The Trustees of The British Museum by BRITISH MUSEUM PRESS

First published 1985
Second edition 1999

Published by British Museum Press
A division of The British Museum Company Ltd
46 Bloomsbury Street, London WC1B 3QQ

A catalogue record for this book is available from
the British Library

ISBN 0 7141 2138 X

Designed by Martin Richards
Typeset in Monotype Bembo
Printed in Slovenia
by Korotan

Frontispiece *Dionysos, the god of wine, and his
son Oinopion. Neck amphora signed by Exekias
as potter, and attributed to him as painter. Made
in Athens, 540–530 BC. Ht 41.6 cm. BM Cat.
Vases B210 (reverse of fig. 45)*

CONTENTS

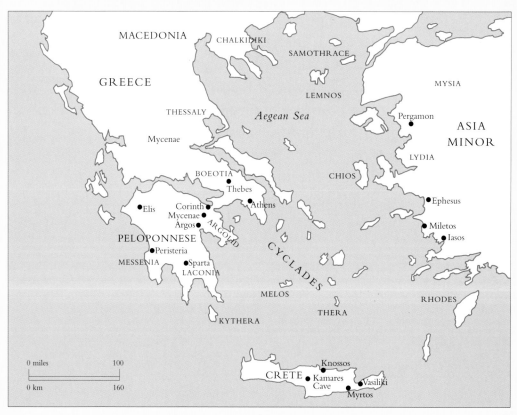

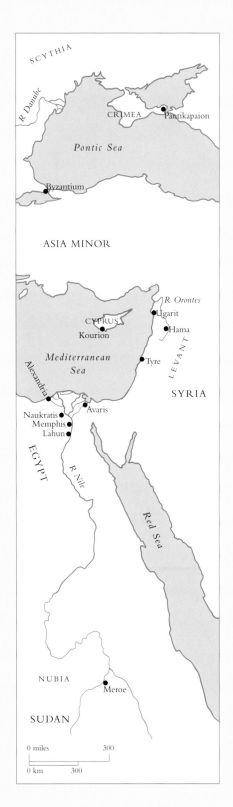

PREFACE

This book is intended to serve not only as a brief introduction to the world of Greek vases but also as a select guide to the collection of the British Museum. Unfortunately, at the time of writing, the vases included here are sadly scattered about the Museum; some are even still in storage. It is hoped, however, in the next few years to make all the vases illustrated here, and many more, visible to all.

As is usual with a general introduction to a subject, this work draws heavily on the studies of other scholars, not least the work of Sir John Beazley on Athenian vase-painters. To these scholars, both past and present, I am deeply indebted. In addition, I should like to thank Dr D. von Bothmer of The Metropolitan Museum of Art in New York and Dr M. Maass of the Badisches Landesmuseum in Karlsruhe for their generous co-operation in reassembling the Brygos Tomb in London forty years after Beazley's study of the group and in time for the centenary of his birth in 1985.

Many colleagues in the British Museum have helped in the production of this book. I should like to mention in particular Brian Cook, Keeper of the Department of Greek and Roman Antiquities, Nigel Williams of the Department of Scientific Research and Conservation, Susan Burch of Office Services, and Ivor Kerslake and James Hendry of Photographic Services. For their support, and that of my wife Korinna, I am very grateful.

To the memory of my mother, Eira

Dyfri Williams May 1984

Preface to Second Edition

It is nearly fifteen years since the first edition of this book was written and the study of Greek pottery has moved on, as have the exhibitions in the British Museum. The whole text has been reviewed, expanded and much revised, although the general chronological structure has been retained. More importantly, the photographic skills of P.E. (Nic) Nicholls have also enabled immense improvements to be made to the illustrations.

Time has also brought new debts to both friends and colleagues; I should like to mention particularly Dr Lucilla Burn and Dr Susan Woodford. I am also very glad to have the chance to thank two private collectors who have very generously loaned significant pieces to the British Museum (figs 23 and 52b). Finally, I should like to pay homage to the Department's international group of friends, the Caryatids, who continue to support all our work in a seemingly endless period of severe financial restraint.

For my father, Roderick

June 1998

INTRODUCTION

The making of pottery from fired clay was the most widespread of all the crafts in ancient times. Every manner of shape could be made and all kinds of functions fulfilled. Both wet and dry materials could be stored in pottery vessels, cooking could be done in them and people could eat and drink from them. Moreover, since the Greeks, like many ancient peoples, not only used pottery but treasured it, it is to be found in sanctuaries and in tombs, as well as in domestic contexts. The only drawback for the owner of pottery, then as now, is its breakability. This is, however, to the advantage of the archaeologist, for broken pottery is, as a result, the most frequently excavated material on ancient sites.

The pottery found in tombs is usually complete, but not always intact, that from settlements and sanctuaries is regularly reduced to isolated fragments. Yet even a small fragment is of interest to an archaeologist, for from a careful study of its decoration and shape its date can be estimated and, therefore, that of the context in which it is found. The importance of ancient Greek vases, however, goes beyond the regular uses to which pottery is put by the archaeologist, for one of their most remarkable features is that they are often decorated with scenes involving human figures, and these can provide valuable insights into ancient Greek customs, beliefs and even fantasies. Finally, Greek vases may frequently be appreciated just for their sheer beauty of form and decoration.

1   MAKING AND PAINTING A GREEK VASE

Kritias, the late fifth-century Athenian politician and poet, claimed that it was Athens 'that invented the potter's wheel and the offspring of clay and kiln, pottery so famous and useful about the house'. Although this claim is probably not true, Athenian clay was one of the finest Greek clays by reason of its excellent working characteristics and its warm orangey-red colour, and it was at Athens that the art of pottery reached its peak. We shall, therefore, anticipate some of the early history of Greek pottery and concentrate first on the technique of Athenian pottery-making and painting.

Clay is essentially weathered rock. Sometimes it is found in its original location, undisturbed, in which case it is called 'primary' clay and is extremely pure. More often in the Mediterranean, however, it has been moved from its original position by glacial action or erosion and deposited elsewhere, together with impurities which may colour it. This is 'secondary' clay. Around Athens the plentiful 'secondary' clay beds are rich in iron and the clay they produce turns an orangey-red when fired. A hill on the island of Aigina, close to Athens, however, is made up of a 'secondary' clay with intrusive sea shells which fires to a yellowish green (fig. 1). The colour of clays and their different impurities enable us to

1 *Dimitris Garis digging out clay on a hill near Mesagros on the island of Aigina. He uses a small pick to cut it out and examine it (author's photograph).*

distinguish between their various places of origin, both by eye and by scientific analysis.

Clay, as it is dug out, is full of foreign bodies which must be removed before it can be used. This was done in ancient times, as it is today, by mixing the clay with water and letting the heavier impurities sink to the bottom. This process of settling ('levigation' or 'elutriation') could be carried out as many times as were necessary in order to obtain the right degree of purity for the form and function of the vessel required.

After the clay was sufficiently purified and the required amount kneaded and prepared (clays might even be mixed), it would be centred on the wheel and drawn up by the potter's deft fingers into whatever shape was desired. The finished vessel was usually made up of separate pieces – feet, handles and spouts. Even the body itself, if it was over 30 cm high, might be made in sections, for clay has a tendency to slump above such a height. These sections and pieces were dried for about twelve hours and then joined together using a clay slip as a glue. On the

2 A potter adding the handle to a cup that stands on his wheel. Interior of a cup made in Athens, about 490 BC; from Saqqara. Diam. of tondo 6.3 cm. BM Cat. Vases B 432

inside of a rather rough Athenian cup we see a potter applying the handle to the cup which stands before him on his wheel (fig. 2). Above, on a shelf, sit some of his finished products (four cups and what looks like a jug), probably drying out before being decorated. Below the potter's feet his dog patiently waits for the end of the day.

After potting came the decoration. Some preliminary sketching was often done before the final painting, but whatever substance was used cannot now be determined since it was burnt off during the firing of the vessel in the kiln. The most we can see is a very faint indentation in the surface of the vase, and even this only seems to occur when the sketch was made before the vase was properly dry. The painting itself was, in fact, done neither with paint nor with glaze, although these terms are often the most convenient. The materials that Athenian potters used to decorate their vessels were nothing more than specially prepared clays. The key colour is the shiny black, which contrasts so well with the warm orangey colour of the fired clay. The black slip, usually

3 Detail of the exterior of a cup showing the birth of Athena; from Vulci. Made in Athens, about 540 BC; attributed to the Phrynos Painter. Ht of figures 4 cm. BM Cat. Vases B 424

called black glaze or gloss, consisted, at Athens, of a more finely purified, almost concentrated, form of the regular clay which by an ingenious firing process turned black in the kiln, in contrast to the orangey-red body. Additional colours were also used, especially from the seventh century BC onwards. The two most common of these are a purplish red and a yellowish white, both with a matt surface (fig. 3). The purplish red was produced by mixing in red iron oxide pigment (ochre). The white was simply a very pure, 'primary' clay with almost no iron oxide present to colour it on firing. These two colours were fired on in the kiln, but occasionally, at certain times and under certain circumstances, colours were added after firing. These were more fugitive, mineral or vegetable colours that would have burnt off at the temperatures used in the kiln and they included blues, greens, pinks and other matt colours.

The application of these slips and colours was usually done with brushes. Sometimes, however, the lines have a real three-dimensional quality, especially the so-called 'relief line' of the red-figure technique, which has led to a number of suggestions concerning both the implement used and the technique employed – a quill, a bag with a nozzle for extruding the clay like a piping-bag for icing a cake, and a hair or group of hairs laid on the surface and then lifted off. Examination of the form of such lines and how they behave seems to indicate, however, that even these 'relief lines' were made with a brush, probably a brush with long, thin bristles, rather like a modern-day 'rigger' brush used for rendering the rigging in oil-paintings of ships. For this sort of line, however, the consistency of the slip must have been particularly thick. In contrast, we also see thin, golden-brown lines which are a result of deliberately diluting the slip ('dilute glaze lines').

Let us now consider the ingenious firing process that turned the body of a Greek vase red but made the slipped or painted parts black. Unlike modern pottery, ancient Greek pottery was only fired once, but that single firing had three stages. First, the vases were stacked in the upper chamber of the kiln (fig. 4). They were nested one inside another or balanced one on top of each other or on a clay ring, and there is sometimes a reddish ring around the wall of a cup or on the side of a larger vase where such stacking has resulted in a slightly irregular temperature at the point of contact. When the stacking was complete, the fire was lit and the kiln heated up to about 800°C under oxidizing conditions, that is with free access of air. During this first stage the vases in the kiln turned red all over. After the temperature had reached 800°C the atmosphere was changed to a reducing one by introducing green wood into the firing chamber and closing the air vents. While this reducing atmosphere was maintained, the temperature was raised to around 950°C and then allowed to cool down to about 900°C. During this second stage the vessels turned all black. There then followed the third and final stage of the firing process: the vents were opened and the atmosphere returned to an oxidizing one, as the kiln was allowed to cool

4 *Diagram of a kiln, adapted from A. Winter,* Die Antike Glanztonkeramik *(Mainz 1978, p.28); drawing by Susan Bird:* (1) *stoking tunnel;* (2) *firing chamber;* (3) *central post;* (4) *pierced floor;* (5) *stacking chamber;* (6) *spy-hole and hatch;* (7) *removable section of wall to enable loading;* (8) *vent hole;* (9) *cover for stoking tunnel*

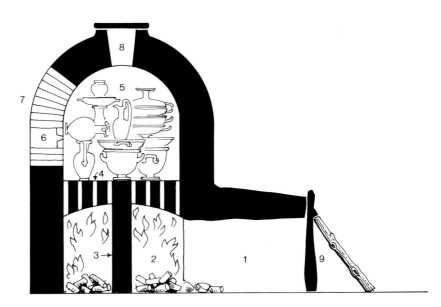

completely. In this final stage the body of the vase turned red again, but the areas painted with black slip remained a glossy black.

This division in colour and texture is caused by the partial vitrification or sintering of the surface of the slipped areas at the moment of highest temperature in the second stage, a sealing of the surface which prevents the re-entry of oxygen and the subsequent return to the red colour in the final stage. This effect was enhanced by the use of potash in the purification process of the clay slip. If by chance the temperature was raised too high in the third phase, say to 1050°C, the oxygen would re-enter and the slipped areas go red again. The successful three-stage firing of an Athenian vase was, therefore, dependent on a precise control of both the atmosphere in the kiln and the temperature. This control was achieved by the use of test or draw pieces inserted through the hatch in the side of the domed kiln, and by experienced observation of the colours to be glimpsed through the spyhole.

There were, however, many things that could go wrong in the kiln and ancient potters seem to have been very superstitious, fearing all sorts of special demons with names like 'Smasher', 'Crasher' and 'Shaker' as is revealed by an anonymous poem, the *Kiln*. Pottery-making was a hard and demanding craft; indeed a popular ancient idiom for 'to work hard' was 'to make pottery'. It was, moreover, a craft that required a great deal of skill and experience. We find, therefore, not only that some ancient potters were probably slaves but also that the craft was passed from father to son (fig. 46) and even to grandson. In three scenes of potters' workshops, one on a Corinthian sixth-century plaque, a second on an Athenian red-figured hydria (water jar) of about 470 BC, and the third on a fifth-century Boeotian black-figure skyphos (drinking cup), a woman is to be seen among the staff. This suggests that in some establishments the whole family might be enlisted – a scenario that recalls modern parallels such as that of Dimitris Garis, shown collecting clay near Mesagros on Aigina (fig. 1), who is himself a fifth-generation potter and has worked with both his mother and wife.

The role of women in potters' workshops in the ancient Greek world, however, is very hard to substantiate. On a Late Bronze Age document from Knossos on Crete a woman is named as a potter (*ke-ra-me-ja*), but there are no certain signatures of female potters or painters from Archaic or Classical contexts. All we have are two names Douris (written Doris) and Kallis, which from their formation might be feminine, but need not be. Douris we know chiefly as a painter (fig. 58), but there are no clues from the iconography of the scenes depicted, nor perhaps should we expect them, for the potential purchaser was all. Kallis, however, is named as potter and dedicator in a scratched inscription (possibly made before firing) on a small fragment (about 470 BC) from the Acropolis at Athens, but we know nothing more of him or her.

The remains of potters' workshops of the sixth and fifth centuries BC that have been discovered in Athens line the major roads that passed out of the city to the northwest through the area known in antiquity as the Kerameikos. The evidence of their debris suggests that workshops actually produced a wide variety of types of objects, which included figured vases, plain black vases, unslipped vases and even lamps. The size and number of such workshops no doubt varied over the centuries: they grew, split, merged and went bankrupt, but such matters are largely a matter of guesswork.

2   THE FIRST FIVE MILLENNIA
FROM NEOLITHIC TO BRONZE AGE

The earliest pottery from the Greek peninsula goes back to the second half of the seventh millennium BC (the Early Neolithic period). This first pottery was handmade, built up from coils and slabs of clay, the final shape being achieved by cutting and scraping the interior and exterior. At first such pottery was plain, its shapes simple and functional. Three types of decoration eventually developed: simple incisions, impressed or relief designs and, when potters could consistently produce a smooth surface, some painted patterns were also attempted. The paint used on these early vases was normally of a mineral composition which, when subjected to a single-stage firing, most probably in a bonfire, turned a matt black or brown. It was only in the sixth millennium BC (Middle Neolithic) that a dark brown lustrous wash was achieved on some vases from southern Greece (Urfirnis Ware); this was in time to develop into the wonderful glossy black slip or glaze so typical of later Athenian pottery. It is important to note that such Middle Neolithic pottery was not only technically sophisticated but was also transported over considerable distances, and not just as containers.

By the late fourth millennium, the beginning of the Early Bronze Age, the range of shapes was enlarged to include 'luxury' vessels, such as those made to hold precious trinkets, thereby reinforcing the impression that pottery was already being produced for trade rather than simply for essential domestic use. On Crete, the most southerly Greek island, which was to play an important role in the early history of the Greek world, an unusual type of handmade pottery occurred in the third millennium BC: it is called Vasiliki Ware after a settlement in eastern Crete where it was first discovered. Here, the vase has been given a lustrous reddish-brown wash and the surface mottled with large darker spots (fig. 5). This rather attractive effect, perhaps intended to imitate the variegated stone vases that were then fashionable, suggests both experimentation with firing techniques, including the control of oxidizing and reducing atmospheres, and the use of reliable kilns.

Excavations at Myrtos on Crete have brought to light some thirty potters' 'mats' – disks of fired clay with slightly convex undersides to aid

5 Opposite *Early Bronze Age Vasiliki Ware bridge-spouted jar with mottled decoration; from Palaikastro. Made on Crete, 2500–2300 BC (EM II). Ht of body 15.2 cm. BM Cat. Vases A 432*

6 Right *Terracotta Minoan wheel-head; from Gournia (Town House). It is seen upside down – the depression in the centre is the socket into which the axle was fitted. Made on Crete, 1700–1500 BC. Diam. 24 cm. GR 1905.6–13.1*

turning and on which the potters built up their vessels. These 'mats' were all found in one place and suggest a communal potting area. It was only around 2000 BC, early in the Middle Bronze Age, that a fast-rotating wheel fixed on a vertical axle fitted into a socket began to be regularly used (fig. 6). This radical advance in ceramic technology co-incided with the development of a palace-based society, especially on Crete, where the earliest wheels have been found, and it is therefore plausible to assume that palace patronage stimulated the introduction of the device.

The results of this technological development differed on Crete and on the mainland. On Crete the potters produced an eggshell-thin ware (Kamares Ware), decorated with white and red paints, and sometimes even yellow, on a shiny black ground. Designs were vivid and well related to the shapes on which they occurred, as is shown even by a modest cup (fig. 7, right). On the mainland, however, the fast wheel brought added crispness to the elaborately turned profiles of the plain burnished or polished ware, which had now become the standard pottery.

Alongside this plain, metallic-looking wheel-made pottery there arose on the mainland around 1900 BC a hand-made dark-on-light ware decorated with a matt paint on a buff-coloured surface. This rather retrogressive step was perhaps the result of migrations from the East: indeed, we see the decorative scheme pass through the Cyclades to the island of Aigina, where clay like that from Garis's hill was used (fig. 1), and finally to the mainland. The most imaginative use of the technique,

7 Opposite above
(a) *Egyptian imitation of a Middle Bronze Age Kamares Ware cup with crinkled rim and impressed decoration; from Lahun (Egypt). Made in Egypt, 1850–1800 BC. Ht 7.7 cm. BM Cat. Vases A 562*

(b) *Middle Bronze Age Kamares Ware cup (handle missing); from Knossos. Made on Crete, 1950–1850 BC (MM I B). Ht 4.5 cm. BM Cat. Vases A 477*

8 Opposite below
(a) *Middle Bronze Age Matt-Painted jug decorated with birds; from Knossos ('Temple Repositories'). Made in the Cyclades, 1700–1550 BC (MC). Ht as preserved 37 cm. BM Cat. Vases A 360*

(b) *Middle Bronze Age Matt-Painted jug; from Melos. Made in the Cyclades, 1850–1700 BC (MC). Ht 39.8 cm. BM Cat. Vases A 342*

however, continued to be in the Cyclades, the so-called Cycladic White Ware, as a fine jug from Melos demonstrates (fig. 8, right). Here we see how the potter has turned a simple narrow-necked jug into something both elegant and remarkably human by tilting the neck back, adding a pair of small breasts to the upper body and painting in the midst of an abstract, moustache-like pattern a single human eye.

The first half of the second millennium BC that saw the rise of the first great palaces on the island of Crete also witnessed the establishment of Minoan trading posts or colonies on islands like Aigina and Kythera, through which influence passed to the Greek mainland, and across the Aegean on Samothrace to the north and on Rhodes and Kos to the east, and even on the coast of Asia Minor at Miletos and Iasos. Important trading contacts were made with Ugarit on the coast of Syria, whence Cretan goods are recorded as passing on to Mari on the Euphrates, and with Avaris in the Nile Delta and Lahun further up that great, life-giving river, where exotic Cretan Kamares Ware was even imitated (fig. 7, left).

Towards the end of the First Palace period on Crete the inventiveness of the best Kamares Ware was diminishing, perhaps as inspiration dimmed or as the availability of luxury vessels in metal or other expensive materials rose. Dark-on-light style pottery gained popularity in the Second Palace period (c.1700-1450 BC) and a standardized range of motifs, including spirals, sprays (fig. 12 c) and foliate patterns took hold, being imitated on the mainland and in the Cyclades. An unusual group of about a dozen large jugs (fig. 8, left), made on the Cyclades and decorated with birds and discs, was actually found, together with faience cult figures, in special cists cut in the floor of a room on the west side of the palace of Knossos, named the 'Temple Repositories' by Sir Arthur Evans, the excavator of the palace. By about 1500 BC some particularly elaborate pottery was being made on Crete itself. The plant, marine (fig. 9, left) and geometric motifs probably echoed developments in fresco painting on the walls of the palaces, while elements of the shapes may have reflected vessels of metal or stone. The products of these Cretan palatial workshops were both widely exported and even imitated on the mainland (fig. 9, right).

The contents of the Shaft Graves at Mycenae in the Argolid and the tholos tombs at Peristeria in Messenia bear witness to the rise in wealth and power on the mainland too. At some point during this period, however, the Cycladic island of Thera, essentially a huge volcano, suffered a

9 (a) *Late Bronze Age rhyton with an octopus against a net and in a rocky seascape; from Palaikastro. Made on Crete, 1500–1450 BC (LM IB). Ht 30.5 cm. BM Cat. Vases A 650*

(b) *Late Bronze Age Marine Style flat alabastron with an argonaut in a rocky seascape; probably from Egypt. Made on the Greek mainland, 1500–1450 BC (LH II A). Ht 11.5 cm. BM Cat. Vases A 651*

devastating eruption. The centre of the island was blown out and the remaining land covered in a deep mantle of hot ash and smouldering pumice. The exact date of this catastrophe is still debated, as is the extent of its physical and political consequences. The eruption is normally placed about 1530 BC and modern excavations have revealed a whole section of this Cycladic town, with buildings standing to two stories, but it seems that the inhabitants had warning of the disaster. The British Museum possesses a small Late Cycladic jug (fig. 10), discovered in 1866 some 3 metres down in the layer of pumice that similarly engulfed the farmstead on the islet of Therasia, on the western side of Thera.

Some while later, towards 1450 BC, there was a series of destructions at most Minoan sites that marked the end of the Second Palace period, a period that had seen a considerable 'minoanization' of many arts and crafts throughout the Aegean. Into this vacuum stepped the mainlanders. The effect on the pottery was a tendency towards a convergence of styles: on Crete we see at first large impressive vases with grandiose yet stiff decoration (fig. 11, right), but during the fourteenth century there was increasing simplification and standardization throughout the Aegean, as political control began to centre on the city of Mycenae.

The potting of these late Mycenaean vases is often very fine, with clean-lined shapes. Decorative motifs were still ultimately derived from fifteenth-century Cretan plant and marine designs, but all now stylized and simplified. The curving bands and lines on a splendid jug (fig. 11, left) might suggest waving grasses but their torsion and swelling power-

10 *Late Bronze Age Matt-Painted juglet decorated with eyes and a necklace; from Therasia (Farmstead, Room E). Made in the Cyclades, 1550–1500 BC (LC I). Ht 12.5 cm. GR 1926.4–10.9*

11 (a) *Late Bronze Age jug with cut away neck; from Maroni (tomb 5) on Cyprus. Made on the Greek mainland, 1350–1300 BC (LH III A2). Ht 31 cm. BM Cat. Vases C 579*

(b) *Late Bronze Age globular flask; from Maroni (tomb 18). Made on Crete, 1400–1350 BC (LM III A1). Ht 40.5 cm. BM Cat. Vases C 563*

fully emphasize the contours of the body and neck of the vessel, while two high-stemmed cups receive marine motifs that similarly seek to echo their tall, elegant shape (fig. 12 b and d). A simpler drinking vessel, a small cylindrical mug, is decorated in a much fussier manner with birds (upper zone) and fish (lower zone), although the inclusion of a religious motif, the so-called 'horns of consecration', adds an unexpected dimension. This mug's shape is also found in gold and silver in some rich mainland tombs, reminding us of a largely missing link. The plain goblet in the same illustration (fig. 12 e) belongs to a different class of metallic imitations. Here the surface was once covered with a tinned slip, in close imitation of a silver vessel. Such tinned cups have been found in graves on the mainland together with actual silver examples.

Palace control of the main centres meant that a palatial bureaucracy was born and the need for keeping records led to the development of a writing system. Linear A is known from the eighteenth century BC on Crete, while its successor, Linear B, is found in palaces on Crete and the mainland. Linear B is essentially syllabic and the language Greek, but the

12 From left to right (a) *Late Bronze Age cylindrical cup with two zones: the upper one has birds flanking a pair of sacred horns, the lower fishes; from Ialyssos (tomb 38) on Rhodes. Made on the Greek mainland, 1350–1300 BC (LH III A2). Ht 8.2 cm. BM Cat. Vases A 846*

(b) *Late Bronze Age high-stemmed cup with a stylized octopus (or cuttlefish); from Ialyssos (tomb 26). Made on the Greek mainland, 1350–1300 BC (LH III A2). Ht 21 cm. BM Cat. Vases A 870*

(c) *Late Bronze Age cup with leafy sprays; from Knossos. Made on Crete, 1450–1400 BC (LM II). Diam. 10 cm. BM Cat. Vases A 633*

(d) *Late Bronze Age high-stemmed kylix with stylized murex shells; from Ialyssos (tomb 12). Made on the Greek mainland, 1350–1300 BC (LH III A2). Ht 15.2 cm. BM Cat. Vases A 868*

(e) *Late Bronze Age stemmed cup once covered with a tinned slip; from Ialyssos (tomb 5). Made on the Greek mainland, 1350–1300 BC (LH III A2). Ht 14.7 cm. BM Cat Vases A 860*

tablets also bear some ideograms for vase shapes. An example is the stirrup-handled jar, nearly two thousand of which are listed. A typical, real stirrup-handled storage jar is a piece from Kourion on Cyprus that is decorated with an octopus on each side (fig. 13). This vase was made in western Crete, but has incised marks on the handles that suggest the Cypriot sign for 'T'.

Smaller versions of the stirrup jar shape are almost 'type fossils' of Late Bronze Age Greece. They were exported all over the Mediterranean, especially to Egypt (fig. 14, right) and the Near East, and no doubt contained pleasantly perfumed oil, while the larger domestic versions probably held plainer oil or wine. Such small stirrup jars were even imitated in Egypt in attractive blue faience (fig. 14, left) and in white calcite (Egyptian alabaster). They help to reveal that Mycenaean trade routes were clearly built on

13 *Large stirrup-handled storage jar decorated with an octopus; from Kourion (tomb 50) on Cyprus (incorporating fragments presented by the University of Philadelphia Museum). Made on Crete, 1300–1200 BC (LM III B). Ht 46 cm. BM Cat Vases C 501*

the very profitable ones developed by the Minoans to the south and east, and that western connections were also added, for such pottery has been found on Sicily, in Italy as far north as the Po valley, on Sardinia, and even as far west as Spain.

Rather different in scale and decoration, however, is a series of kraters (mixing bowls) in a pictorial style. The earliest examples depict birds and fish, but from about 1375 BC we find human figures in chariots. This is the first sustained use of human figures on the pottery of Greece; the idea was probably borrowed from wall-painting, a medium in which the depiction of men and women was clearly felt to be more appropriate. On a small krater we see two chariots loosely disposed across the upper

14 (a) *Egyptian imitation in faience of a Mycenaean stirrup jar. Made in Egypt, New Kingdom, about 1350 BC. Ht 6.7 cm. EA 1901.6–8.146 (35413)*

(b) *Late Bronze Age stirrup jar; from Gurob in the Fayum, Egypt (coffin of Res). Made on the Greek mainland, about 1300 BC (LH III A2/B). Ht 12 cm. BM Cat. Vases A 987*

15 *Late Bronze Age krater with chariots; from Maroni on Cyprus. Made on the Greek mainland, 1350–1300 BC (LH III A2). Ht 25.8 cm. GR 1911.4–28.1*

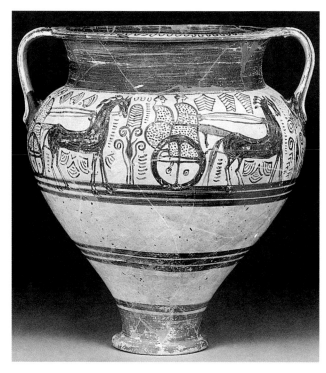

frieze (fig. 15). There is a naive charm to the painting that avoids the greater pretension of the frescoes from the mainland palaces.

Around 1200 BC these palaces were destroyed. Many sites were abandoned and there seems to have been some consequent restructuring of Mycenaean society. As a result, the uniform Mycenaean pottery style began to fragment into a number of local styles and there was an initial decline in the repertoire of designs. Towards the end of the twelfth century, however, there was something of a recovery and three main styles may be observed: a loose, linear style with simple motifs (the Granary Style), a more complex style with densely packed ornaments (the Close Style, fig. 16 c), and a debased pictorial style. On some vases at this time the regular reddish glaze gives way to a shiny black, as on fig. 16 a, prefiguring the regular colour of the glaze in the next millennium.

This recovery was not to last and the decorative repertoire retracted into simple linear designs or even plain monochrome slips. There were further declines in the size of the population throughout

Greece and the islands and deepening isolation. The pottery, now termed Sub-Mycenaean and Sub-Minoan, retains old, well-established shapes, with the stirrup jar still popular everywhere (fig. 16 b and e), the small amphora well-liked in Athens but less so in the Peloponnese (fig. 16 d). The potting is often rough and careless.

16 Left to right (a) *Late Bronze Age stirrup jar. Made on the Greek mainland, 1190–1130 BC (LH IIIC). Ht 14.5 cm. GR 1998.2–14.1*

(b) *Sub-Minoan stirrup jar; said to be from Argos. Made in Crete, 1100–1050 BC. Ht 11 cm. GR 1939.10–11.1*

(c) *Late Bronze Age Close Style stirrup jar; from Ialyssos (Rhodes). Made on the Greek mainland, 1150–1100 BC (LH IIIC Middle). Ht 21.5 cm. BM Cat. Vases A 931*

(d) *Sub-Mycenaean belly-handled amphora; probably from Athens. Made in Athens, 1100–1050 BC. Ht 10.8 cm. BM Cat. Vases A 1093*

(e) *Sub-Mycenaean stirrup jar; probably from Athens. Made in Athens, 1050–1000 BC. Ht 19.7 cm. BM Cat. Vases A 1097*

3 FROM 1000 BC TO 700 BC
THE GEOMETRIC RENAISSANCE

After a period of isolation, the Greek people and their potters began to look abroad again, as recent finds from Lefkandi on Euboea have revealed: the Submycenaean slumber was broken and in due course a new beginning was made. This renaissance began at Athens in the later eleventh century BC and is marked by the appearance of so-called 'Protogeometric' pottery (c.1025–900 BC). Production techniques seem to have improved, for the clay appears more carefully prepared, and the slip (now always black) more lustrous as a result of more thorough refining and higher firing temperatures. In general, new shapes appear while old ones tighten their contours. The dark-on-light scheme of the Mycenaean period is gradually replaced by an overall dark-ground scheme punctuated by bands or panels of decoration. There are also new decorative motifs, including cross-hatched diamonds and triangles, chequerboards, dog-tooth, zigzag and groups of opposed diagonals, but most remarkable of all are the sets of circles and semicircles, rendered with geometrical exactness thanks to a new device, an Athenian invention, the multiple brush fitted to one arm of a compass. It was also during the tenth century that the first attempts at figured decoration were once again made, although these only comprise some small horses on Athenian vases, a pair of archers on a tiny hydria (water jar) from Lefkandi and a pair of hunters on a krater (bowl) from Knossos.

Two Protogeometric vases show us something old and something new (fig. 17). Both shapes, the belly-handled amphora (storage jar) and the neck-handled amphora have Mycenaean origins, but the potting is now wonderfully sharp. The triple wavy-line decoration on the former is old too, but the way it is set in a panel and framed by stitch-like zigzags has not been seen before, nor has the chequerboard. Similarly, the neck-handled amphora still retains the light-ground effect of its Mycenaean predecessors, but it now shows off the possibilities of the compass and multiple brush to startling effect.

The clarity of shape and decoration suggests a new self-respect among the potters of Athens that grew in the coming centuries, while it can now be seen that Athenian pottery began to be attractive to

17 (a) *Protogeometric belly-handled amphora; probably from Athens. Made in Athens, 950–900 BC (LPG). Ht 35 cm. BM Cat. Vases A 1123*

(b) *Protogeometric neck-handled amphora, with concentric circles; probably from Athens. Made in Athens, 975–950 BC (MPG-LPG). Ht 43.4 cm. BM Cat. Vases A 1124*

distant buyers, for it is to be found from Northern Greece to Miletos in the east and Crete in the south. Indeed, when Kritias claimed that Athens invented the potter's wheel, he and his fifth-century contemporaries were probably looking back to just this period and to grand vessels like the giant jar, fig. 18.

Around 900 BC there was a change in the repertoire of decorative motifs that heralds the beginning of the so-called Geometric period (c.900-700 BC): the large compass-drawn circular elements were replaced by two new rectilinear forms, the maeander or Greek key pattern and the battlement, often set in rectangular panels. From the Early Geometric period at Athens (c.900-850 BC) we may take a jug that displays both the old stitch-like zigzag pattern and the new maeander motif on its neck (fig. 19). It is, of course, the maeander that is to characterize Geometric art for us.

The beginning of the Middle Geometric period is marked in Athens by a number of tombs that reveal an immense surge in wealth, as measured by the presence in them of gold jewellery and foreign trinkets.

18 *Large Protogeometric pyxis; from Athens. Made in Athens, 950–900 BC (LPG). Ht 48.3 cm. GR 1950.2–28.3*

19 *Early Geometric oinochoe; probably from Athens. Made in Athens, 875–850 BC (EGII). Ht 29.9 cm. GR 1950.2–28.2*

The vases that accompanied these aristocratic burials are of consummate quality. Some are of monumental splendour and served as grave-markers set above ground: the belly handled-amphora over the tombs of women, the pedestalled krater over the men's, a rigid division by gender that was already beginning to be made in the tenth century BC (cf. fig. 20). Some of these particularly large vessels, both amphorai and krater, were widely exported and imitated (fig. 20, right). Fragments have been found as far east as the Levant, at the royal Israelite capital of Samaria, at Phoenician Tyre and in the royal quarter at Hama on the Orontes, but the most remarkable example of this apparent gift-exchange system is a fragment from the far west, from Huelva, on the Atlantic coast of Spain, beyond the 'Pillars of Hercules'.

During the Middle Geometric period (c.850-760 BC) the enthusiasm for new geometric patterns began to drive back the black, so beloved of earlier generations. An oinochoe (fig. 21, left) demonstrates this with its multiple horizontal bands, but the pair of birds on the shoulder also point to an increase in the number of animals, such as horses, stags and

20 (a) *Middle Geometric belly-handled amphora (base missing); probably from Athens. Made in Athens, 850–800 BC (MG I). Ht 47 cm. GR 1977.12–7.6*

(b) *Middle Geometric pedestalled krater; from Kamiros on Rhodes. Made on Rhodes, 800–750 BC (MG). Ht 55.5 cm. GR 1861.4–25.51*

dogs, that appear next to the complex abstract designs. Human figures are still extremely rare – there is a mourning woman on an Attic pedestalled krater, and a number of more complex scenes on the strongly oriental products of Crete, including goddesses and a man attacked by lions. On a smaller vase, a circular toilet box (pyxis) with lid, the surface is almost entirely covered with narrow bands of linear ornament (fig 21, right). It is a new shape that appears at this time and becomes standard for the Geometric period: indeed, the pyxis is a common gift both in tombs, especially those of women, and in sanctuaries. On this example the knobbed handle takes the form of a second, miniature pyxis – on other Geometric vases the handle knob sometimes takes the form of a shape related in function or a special symbol, such as a horse or a beehive.

Around 770 BC Athens entered a new phase of artistic revolution. The most important change was the sudden development of ambitious figured scenes. The subjects represented include fights on land and sea, processions of warriors and chariots, and ceremonies concerned with the dead. The painting was essentially conceptual – the artist drew what he knew to be there rather than what he could actually see (fig. 22). Each part of the body was given its most diagnostic view: head in profile, chest frontal and triangular (the female breasts project from the sides),

21 (a) *Middle Geometric oinochoe with birds on the neck; probably from Athens. Made in Athens, 800–760 BC (MG II). Ht 32.7 cm. GR 1977.12–7.50*

(b) *Middle Geometric pyxis with a handle in the form of another pyxis. Made in Athens, 850–800 BC (MG I). Diam. 19 cm. GR 1913.11–13.2*

22 *Detail of a Late Geometric pitcher showing mourners at the laying-out of the dead. Made in Athens, 720–700 BC (LG IIb). Ht of figures 5.8 cm. GR 1912.5–22.1*

and legs in profile with prominent buttocks and calves. These schematic silhouettes seem to mark a new beginning for figure-painting in Greece, but they do not necessarily represent the first naive attempts of an artist who had never seen figure-painting before, for new excavations are continually providing evidence of contacts with cultures that retained a tradition of representing figures in a variety of media.

Such complex Geometric figured scenes are concentrated on monumental grave markers, well over a metre high, and are combined with the most meticulous geometric patterns. More than sixty per cent of the known examples in the first decade of their production are the work of one craftsman and his assistants, active in a single workshop, now known as the Dipylon Workshop after Athens' double gateway next to the cemetery where many were discovered. Given their size and complexity, these must have been special commissions placed by aristocratic families. On some, the work of more than one hand may be distinguished, perhaps the result of the scale of the vase and the complexity of its decoration, as well as the need to finish the commission in time for the third day after death when the body had to be buried. The Dipylon Workshop also produced a variety of other, relatively smaller vases, all outstanding in the precision of the drawing of their geometric patterning (fig. 23).

The Dipylon Painter's workshop was succeeded in the following two decades by three others that largely followed his lead. From then on, however, until the end of the century, there was an explosion in the

23 *Late Geometric neck-amphora; probably from Athens. Made in Athens, about 750 BC (LG I); attributed to the Dipylon Painter. Ht 67 cm. On loan from Stanford Place.*

number of workshops, producing largely minor works and on a much smaller scale. Nevertheless, it was during this time that occasional scenes with seemingly mythological subjects are first to be found. For example, on a large spouted krater, attributed to the so-called Sub-Dipylon Group, is a remarkable representation of a mighty oared ship, filled with oarsmen poised for the command to pull (fig. 24). A man is about to board, but as he does so he grips the wrist of a woman, who stands behind him. This may be Paris abducting Helen, or, perhaps more probably, Theseus escaping from Crete with Ariadne, for the wreath that she is holding could then be the 'garland of light' with which, according to some versions of the story, she lit Theseus' path through the Labyrinth. Such ambiguity is typical of the scenes on Late Geometric vases that appear to be mythological: the artists seem reluctant to break with the generalized approach to narrative that they had developed. With the seventh century, however, such barriers are broken down and mythological scenes can be more explicit.

Many other Greek city-states and regions produced Geometric pottery – Argos, Boeotia, Corinth, Euboea, the Cyclades, Crete and the eastern Greek islands and cities hugging the coastline of Asia Minor (fig. 25). These are distinguishable by their clay, by their shapes and by their decoration. In many areas by the middle of the eighth century the earlier stylistic dependence on Athens had waned and there were more interrelations among the local schools themselves. We can also see connections with non-Greek areas, as in the case of the Rhodian flask

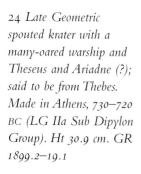

24 *Late Geometric spouted krater with a many-oared warship and Theseus and Ariadne (?); said to be from Thebes. Made in Athens, 730–720 BC (LG IIa Sub Dipylon Group). Ht 30.9 cm. GR 1899.2–19.1*

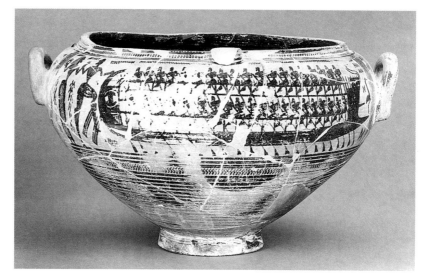

25 Clockwise from back left (a) *Melian Late Geometric stand. Made on Melos, 750–700 BC (LG).*
Ht 26 cm. GR 1837.10–18.1

(b) *Argive Late Geometric pyxis. Made in Argos, 750–730 BC (LG I). Ht 25.5 cm. GR 1865.12–14.11*
(contains burnt bones, fragments of glass, amber and bronze)

(c) *Rhodian Late Geometric flask; from Kamiros (child's tomb on the Acropolis). Made on Rhodes, 740–690 BC*
(LG). Ht 24 cm. GR 1864.10–7.1582

(d) *Corinthian Late Geometric kyathos; from Melos. Made in Corinth, 750–720 BC (LG). Diam. 10.5 cm.*
GR 1842.7–28.824

(e) *Euboean Late Geometric cup. Made on Euboea, 750–710 BC (LG). Diam. 7 cm. GR 1970.9–11.2*

(f) *Boeotian Late Geometric kantharos; said to be from Thebes. Made in Boeotia, 740–690 BC (LG).*
Ht 13.4 cm. GR 1910.10–13.1

(g) *Cretan Late Geometric lekythos; said to be from Athens. Made on Crete, 740–700 BC (LG). Ht 11.5 cm.*
GR 1852.7–7.4

which is of Cypriot shape. Their products also chart the adventurous-
ness of their peoples, such as the Euboeans who were the first to settle
off the coast of central Italy on the island of Pithekoussai and seem to
have been particularly influential in the trade with the Levantine coast,
for in both areas we find exported Euboean works and in central Italy
even groups of emigrant Euboean potters. Indeed, one of these migrant
Euboeans has left us our very first signature of a potter, fragmentary
though it be: it reads [. . .]*inos mepoiese* ([. . .]inos made me).

The products of none of these local schools, however, was as widely
exported as Attic and none had such a prolific figured style. Indeed, one
of the schools most resistant to figured decoration was that of Corinth.
Here simple linear decoration predominated, emphasizing the extremely fine potting that her craftsmen were able to achieve. Two vases, which
date from around 700 BC or soon after and are said to come from a single tomb at Kyme (modern Cuma) in central Italy, show both these

26 (a) *Early
Protocorinthian aryballos;
from Cuma (Italy). Made
on Pithekoussai (Italy),
about 700 BC. Ht 7.5 cm.
GR 1950.1–24.2*

(b) *Early Protocorinthian
kotyle; from Cuma
(Italy). Made in Corinth,
about 700 BC. Ht 8.5 cm.
GR 1950.1–24.1*

characteristics admirably (fig. 26). Although their potting and the style
of their decoration suggest that they were made by Corinthians, only
the deep cup (kotyle) was actually made at Corinth. The redder clay of
the round scent-bottle (aryballos) reveals that it was made on the island
of Pithekoussai just off the coast opposite Kyme: the addition of a pale
slip was intended to make it look like an authentic Corinthian product.

Once the Euboean colony on the island of Pithekoussai was well
established, there seems to have been a move to settle on the mainland
at Kyme. At about the same time a number of Corinthian potters
arrived, following in the footsteps of the Euboeans, perhaps to gain
closer access to the new markets in Italy. The turn of Corinth had come.

4 THE SEVENTH CENTURY BC
CORINTH LEADS THE WAY

The seventh century is often referred to as the Orientalizing period, taking its name from the influx of Near Eastern decorative motifs in art. Actual contacts with the Near East had in fact been renewed as early as the end of the eleventh century, at least to judge from the oriental trinkets found in tombs at Lefkandi. Sporadic contact had continued during the succeeding centuries including the move to Crete of a group of oriental bronzesmiths. Indeed, this contact had culminated by the middle of the eighth century in the development of the art of writing, which harnessed the Phoenician script to the Greek language.

In the world of Greek pottery the seventh century belonged to Corinth. Protocorinthian, as we call Corinthian pottery in the earlier seventh century BC, was now becoming a popular export item, especially the small aryballoi that held perfumed oil. This extra demand, together perhaps with new overseas contacts, caused changes in Corinthian vase-painting. Suddenly the domination of linear decoration was broken and both figures and new oriental-looking motifs were introduced. On a small rounded aryballos (fig. 27, left), dating from the beginning of the seventh century (Early Protocorinthian), we find, in addition to some animals, two piratical-looking figures, one a warrior with shield, helmet, spear and sword, the other a figure on horseback. In the field are new decorative patterns, some strongly curvilinear, especially that just beyond the horse. Most of the drawing is done in outline in contrast to the traditional Geometric silhouettes, but there is also the tentative use of a new idea, that of scratching with a fine point through the black slip to the pale clay below. It can be seen on the diamond between the two figures and, on the other side of the vase, on the dappled skin of a stag. This technique of incising details with a point is known in bronze-working and in ivory-carving, both of which arts flourished in Corinth at this time, and its use by vase-painters may have been borrowed from their fellow craftsmen. From its use on vases like this aryballos, however, it seems that the technique may first have been employed to facilitate the making of fine markings on dark areas – only gradually did artists realize its full potential.

This technique of incision came to fruition towards the middle of the seventh century BC, when it was used for all interior markings of black silhouettes and a purplish red was added to highlight certain areas – this is the so-called 'black-figure' technique. Although the finest Middle Protocorinthian work was done on a miniature scale (fig. 27, right), the occasional bolder scheme was attempted, as on a splendid kotyle (deep cup) from Rhodes (fig. 28, left). Here the lithe, eager form of a hound has been transformed into a tightly contoured balance of dark masses, enlivened by a special polychrome effect, for, although the lower part of the neck has been given a coating of the regular purplish red, the upper section has been coated in a warm yellow. Beside the kotyle stands a larger than normal aryballos (fig. 28, right), dating to about 650 BC (Late Protocorinthian), also found in a tomb on Rhodes. There are three miniature friezes of animals, including lions, dogs, boars and a bull. The painting is superbly sharp; the animals are proud, kingly creatures, suggesting the painter's modern sobriquet, the Head-in-the-Air Painter. The precise dot-rosette filling ornaments are typical of Protocorinthian

27 (a) *Early Protocorinthian aryballos with warrior and squire. Made in Corinth, about 690 BC; attributed to the Evelyn Painter. Ht 6.8 cm. GR 1969.12–15.1*

(b) *Middle Protocorinthian alabastron; from Kamiros, Rhodes. Made in Corinth, 660–650 BC. Ht 5.7 cm. GR 1860.2–1.30*

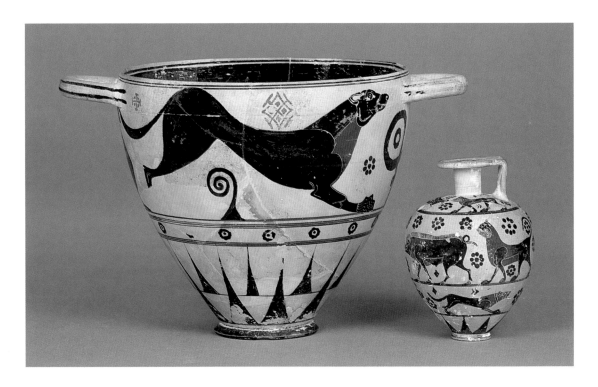

28 (a) *Middle Protocorinthian kotyle; from Kamiros, Rhodes. Made in Corinth, 670–650 BC; attributed to the Hound Painter. Ht 18.2 cm. GR 1860.4–4.18*

(b) *Late Protocorinthian aryballos; from Kamiros. Made in Corinth, about 650–640 BC; attributed to the Head-in-the-Air Painter. Ht 12.8 cm. GR 1860.4–4.16*

vase-painting, while the rays around the base first occur in the seventh century under oriental influence.

Besides such friezes of animals we occasionally meet mythological scenes, especially those centring on Herakles, but on the most elaborate pieces there are complex battle scenes that do not seem to have specific mythological settings. Thus, into the main frieze of a remarkable aryballos (fig. 29), only 6.8 cm tall, are packed seventeen struggling warriors, pushing and thrusting with their spears, their shields decked with vivid blazons. This piece, like the other similarly complex fight scenes by the same painter, known as the Chigi Painter, belongs to a time in Corinth's history when a long-established aristocracy was suddenly replaced by a tyranny, and when a new method of fighting began to gain widespread acceptance. This method involved lines of heavily armed infantry (hoplites) fighting, as the seventh-century poet Tyrtaios described it, 'foot to foot, shield to shield, crest to crest, helmet to helmet, chest to chest, grasping your sword or long spear'. Such battle scenes on vases may perhaps reflect this period of violence and change.

Beneath the frieze of struggling hoplites is a horse-race, and in the lowest zone is a hare-hunt with the hunter hiding behind a stylized bush. The lion's-head spout is rather impractical for a scent-bottle and

29 *Protocorinthian aryballos with lion's head spout and three decorative friezes: a fight, a horse-race and a hare-hunt; said to be from Thebes. Made in Corinth, about 640 BC; attributed to the Chigi Painter. Ht 6.8 cm. GR 1889.4–18.1*

*30 Early Wild Goat Style
standed dinos showing two
goats flanking a stylized
'tree of life'; from
Kamiros, Rhodes.
Probably made on
Rhodes, 670–650 BC. Ht
15.2 cm. GR 1860.2–1.16*

the piece was no doubt intended as a special vase for dedication in a
sanctuary or as an offering for the dead. The idea of such a head or protome is ultimately of oriental origin; it appears on a number of other
early seventh-century vases, which imitate metal forms.

Attached near the rim of a miniature standed cauldron, or dinos, we
see two fully modelled ram's heads (fig. 30). Animal protomes were frequently attached to bronze dinoi in the Near East and the idea was
taken up by the Greeks, who not only imitated the idea in pottery but
actually produced their own bronze dinoi, which they frequently decorated with griffin protomes. The painting on the pottery dinos is typical of the Greek centres along the coast of Asia Minor in the seventh
century – the style is often called the 'Wild Goat Style' after its favourite
animal. All work is done in silhouette and outline; no use is made of
incision. At its best, as here, this pottery is cheerfully, if naively, attractive.
Subsidiary ornaments show much contact with the Near East: the pal-
mette bushes, the rope-like guilloche and the rays on the foot. Later, it

seems that one of the most important production centres of Wild Goat Style was Miletos, although there were workshops on Chios and Rhodes, and at Ephesos and Samos.

A most remarkable late seventh-century East Greek work, however, deserves particular mention, the so-called Euphorbos plate (fig. 31), for it is the only surviving East Greek vase with a heroic scene, the only piece with inscribed names and the only example of polychromy. Here, within the simple frame of a shield-like plate, the painter has given us a combat from Homer's *Iliad* – Menelaos has killed Euphorbos, and Hektor presses to reclaim the body. The figures are done in outline, but the bare flesh is given a rosy red wash, while dilute brown has been used

31 *East Greek plate with Menelaos and Hektor fighting over the body of Euphorbos; from Kamiros, Rhodes. Probably made on Rhodes, about 600 BC. Diam. 38 cm. GR 1860.4–4.1*

on helmets and garments, and Hektor's shield device relies on incision. The names are written in a Doric dialect, such as that used on Rhodes, yet the letter forms seem for the most part more at home in Argos. Perhaps the vase-painter has copied some other work of art, both figures and inscription. It is intriguing to remember, therefore, that, according to Pausanias, Menelaos dedicated the shield of Euphorbos in the temple of Hera near Argos.

The persistence of the silhouette-and-outline technique, despite Corinthian advances in black-figure, is also to be observed in many other parts of the Greek world, such as Argos, Boeotia and Lakonia. A large jug found on Aigina but made somewhere in the central Cyclades, perhaps on Paros, in the second quarter of the seventh century demonstrates this well (fig. 32, right). Again we have animals rendered in outline with interior markings done with paint rather than a point. The motifs are strongly oriental – the guilloche and rays again, and here even the idea of a lion pulling down a stag – so too, the neck and spout of the vessel, shaped in the form of a griffin protome just like those on bronze dinoi. Elsewhere in the Cyclades there was also a brief vogue for polychrome decoration and one fragment proudly carries the remains of the painter's signature.

The vase in the form of a siren, shown next to the Griffin jug, was found in a tomb on the island of Kythera, off the south coast of the Peloponnese (fig. 32, left). This island had strong connections with Crete, far to the south, for many centuries, and this unusual jug, with its mix of incised feathers and outline and relief human parts, seems to have been made there at the end of the seventh century.

At Athens, the Geometric tradition was particularly slow to break up, no doubt because it had proved so successful, and inroads into the black silhouette were for a long time rather half-hearted. A fine lid in the British Museum belongs late in the first quarter of the seventh century (Early Protoattic, 700-675 BC): horses graze, only their eyes and manes executed in a sort of outline, while there is a foal among them in pure Geometric silhouette (fig. 33). Amid the subsidiary ornament has grown occasional vegetable ornaments, which help us to identify the artist, known as the Analatos Painter, although a small fragment of a votive plaque found on Aigina may preserve part of his real name, perhaps [Lys]onos. A remarkable vase from Incoronata, near Metapontion (modern Metaponto) in South Italy, the main panel of which shows Bellerophon slaying the Chimaera, has been connected with the

32 (a) *Jug in the form of a Siren; from Kythera. Probably made on Crete, about 600 BC. Ht 21.5 cm. BM Cat. Terracottas 1677*

(b) *Jug with a griffin protome as a spout, showing a lion pulling down a stag, and a horse; from Aigina. Made on Paros (?), 675–650 BC. Ht 41.5 cm. GR 1873.8–20.385*

33 Right *Early Protoattic lid from a large standed bowl, decorated with horses and a foal; probably from Athens. Made in Athens, about 690–680 BC; attributed to the Analatos Painter. Diam. 25.8 cm. GR 1977.12–11.9*

34 Below *Middle Protoattic krater (foot missing) showing two lions; from Athens. Made in Athens, about 660–650 BC. Preserved ht 25 cm. GR 1842.7–28.827*

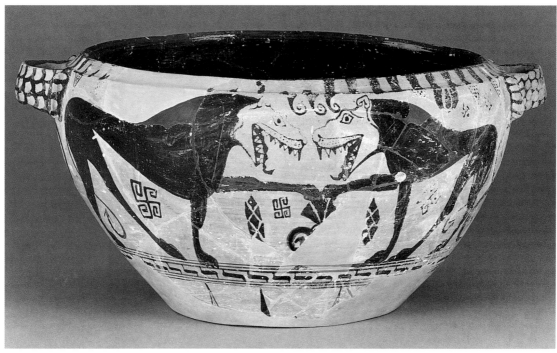

Analatos Painter's hand and may well indicate that he actually emigrated west at the end of his career.

By the middle of the seventh century (Middle Protoattic, 675-650 BC) some significant changes have taken place. Not only do potters once again produce large shapes that were used as tomb markers, but we also find some tentative incision for toes, beards and the like, and also some added white. For example, a large krater, sadly lacking its foot, is decorated with two tooth-laden lions which have outline faces but silhouette bodies (fig. 34). There is no incision; instead, thin white lines have been applied to mark the wavy edges of the manes and on the paws to mark the claws, while alternate teeth have been filled with white. The overall effect is very different from contemporary Corinthian work, even when it is not miniaturistic. All is angular and oversized; Corinthian artists display much more sensitivity to the structure of the animals they draw, making their contours sweep and swell.

Athenian vases of the early seventh century BC are rarely found outside Athens and its surrounding countryside. By contrast, Corinthian products reached as far afield as Syria, Asia Minor and Italy. In the last quarter of the century they are also found further north on the northern coast of the Black Sea and even over the Alps; they are known from the first Greek trading centre in Egypt, that at Naukratis on the Nile Delta, along the coast of north Africa at Carthage and even in Spain. Corinthian artists at this period were still covering their vases with friezes of animals, but their sense of form was beginning to fade and even the contrast between beasts and filling ornaments is lost as the latter decline into large shapeless blobs. An Early Corinthian (as the style is now called) amphora, although ambitious in terms of number, demonstrates this all too well (fig. 35, right): frieze after frieze of square, stubby creatures crowded with frosty snowflakes cover the swelling body. This same manner was to continue until nearly the middle of the following century (fig. 35, left), ever declining, even though other avenues were occasionally tried, as we shall see later. Despite the repetitive nature of such friezes, they had a great impact on many other local fabrics, especially to the west. On Ithaka and Kerkyra we may observe local imitations, but even more prolific workshops appeared in Etruria, Apulia and on Sicily, perhaps encouraged by the appearance of further immigrant craftsmen from Corinth itself.

At Athens the last quarter of the century saw the final adoption of the full black-figure technique from Corinth. A Late Protoattic amphora,

35 Opposite (a) *Middle Corinthian pyxis with female protomes. Made in Corinth, 600–575 BC; attributed to the Honolulu Painter. Ht 21 cm. GR 1873.10–121*

(b) *Early Corinthian amphora with friezes of animals. Made in Corinth, 620–600 BC; attributed to the Walters Painter. Ht 35cm. GR 1914.10–30.1*

36 Right *Late Protoattic amphora with two lions; probably from Athens. Made in Athens, about 620 BC; attributed to the Nettos Painter. Ht 49.7 cm. GR 1874.4–10.1*

seen here from the side, shows the result (fig. 36): it is the work of the last major Protoattic artist and the first Athenian black-figure painter, known as the Nettos Painter. The large lions of the earlier krater have filled out further and developed powerful muscles, delineated now with bold incisions. Red has been added too, highlighting the mane, ear, eye, and muzzle of the lion on the left. Above, pairs of birds peck hungrily at the ground. With these monumental beasts and a full mastery of the craft of potting and painting, the Athenians were all set to move in on the markets developed by Corinth in the seventh century.

5 ATHENS IN THE SIXTH CENTURY BC

THE ACME OF THE BLACK-FIGURE TECHNIQUE

In the earlier chapters reference has sometimes been made to particular painters or workshops, and sometimes names given them such as the Late Geometric Dipylon Workshop, or various Protocorinthian painters like the Chigi Painter or the Head-in-the-Air Painter. Given the very linear style of Greek vase-painting and the large numbers of available pieces, both whole and fragmentary, it is possible to recognize pieces by the same artist even where there is no signature, just as scholars of Renaissance painting have been able to attribute unsigned works to various artists. This sort of work has proved most successful for the material from Athens of the sixth and fifth centuries and the pioneer was Sir John Davidson Beazley, who made this approach his own and succeeded in isolating both major and minor personalities, thus enabling a far deeper understanding of the development of vase-painting in these centuries than has yet been possible in any other period. Anonymous artists are referred to in a variety of ways. Sometimes, for example, the name of the potter is used when he has signed instead of the painter, thus the Amasis Painter; sometimes the artist is given the name of the place where a particular piece was found, hence the Altamura Painter, after Altamura in Italy, or where it now is, as with the Berlin Painter; and sometimes an interesting subject provides a suitable sobriquet.

The beginning of the sixth century saw Athens in crisis: there was both political turbulence and economic instability. In 594 BC Solon was chosen chief archon and commissioned to revise the laws and the constitution. Connected with his reforms were two initiatives that must have affected the pottery industry, although it is virtually impossible for us to observe the results: he welcomed foreign craftsmen and exhorted native Athenians to learn a trade. The first sixth-century vase-painter that we meet is the anonymous Gorgon Painter (fig. 37, left). He was a pupil of the Nettos Painter, but in that tutorship an enormous change occurred, for now there is considerable control and the animals and figures begin to be left to stand boldly free of the distracting subsidiary ornament so beloved of the painters in the Corinthian manner. During the first decades of the sixth century some six pupils carried on the

37 (a) *Oinochoe with a lion; from Nola. Made in Athens, 590–580 BC; attributed to the Gorgon Painter. Ht 26.5 cm. BM Cat. Vases B 33*

(b) *Boeotian alabastron with Artemis as the Mistress of the Animals; said to be from Corinth. Made in Boeotia, 590–580 BC; attributed to the Horse-bird Painter. Ht 23.7 cm. GR 1894.10–31.1*

tradition of the Gorgon Painter. In addition, however, there seem to have been other workshops scattered elsewhere in Attica and neighbouring areas, perhaps in close proximity to a sanctuary, such as Eleusis, or a wealthy cemetery area, such as Vari. In one case, we can actually trace a vase-painter who began work in Athens in a very Corinthian style, managing to export rather ordinary pieces as far afield as Taras (modern Taranto) in South Italy and Smyrna (modern Izmir) in Asia Minor, but who in due course moved into Boeotia, where we call him the Horse-bird Painter (fig. 37, right).

The Gorgon Painter's most famous pupil, however, was the Athenian Sophilos, who has left his name as both potter and painter on a number of vases, including a monumental cauldron or dinos, complete with stand (fig. 38), for in the upper zone, next to one of the columns of a house, is *Sophilos megraphsen* ('Sophilos painted me'). The dinos and its

38 *Dinos with stand decorated with a frieze of gods and goddesses and friezes of animals and mythical creatures. Made in Athens, about 580 BC; signed by Sophilos as painter. Ht 71 cm. GR 1971.11–1.1*

separate stand are covered with friezes of animals, both real and fantastic. The idea is taken over from Corinthian vases, although the arrangement of the animals is now more complex and more fully related to the shape of the vase. The top frieze of the dinos, however, is decorated not with animals but with a procession of human figures (fig. 39). All the participants are named and so the theme is quite clear – the gods have come to celebrate the marriage of mortal Peleus and immortal Thetis. Peleus stands on the right, in front of his house with its red door, white pillars and black antae (projecting wall-ends); he is waiting for the gods as they arrive, holding out a kantharos (high-handled cup) of wine as a sign of welcome. Iris, the messenger goddess, heads the parade and behind her come four goddesses, all connected with marriage in one way or another; they are perhaps looking beyond Peleus to the bride, Thetis, who is hidden behind the closed doors of Peleus' palace. Beyond these comes Dionysos, the god of wine, one hand grasping a vine branch laden with grapes. He seems to talk across the goddesses to Peleus, and it is perhaps to him that the hero is speaking his words of welcome. Dionysos is, in fact, placed over the centre of the elaborate floral in the frieze below, and so stands right in the middle of the front of a vase that was made for the mixing and serving of wine at a feast.

Behind Dionysos comes a stream of other divine guests. There are Hebe, the goddess of youth, in an elaborately woven garment; Cheiron, the wise centaur, part man, part horse, with his catch over his shoulder, a welcome gift for the coming feast; and sundry other goddesses. Around the side of the vase the procession changes and the rest of the gods are paired off in chariots pulled by splendid steeds – there ride Zeus and Hera, Poseidon and Amphitrite, Hermes and Apollo, Athena and Artemis. The procession ends with a slow-moving group of gods, including fish-bodied Okeanos and crippled Hephaistos on his mule.

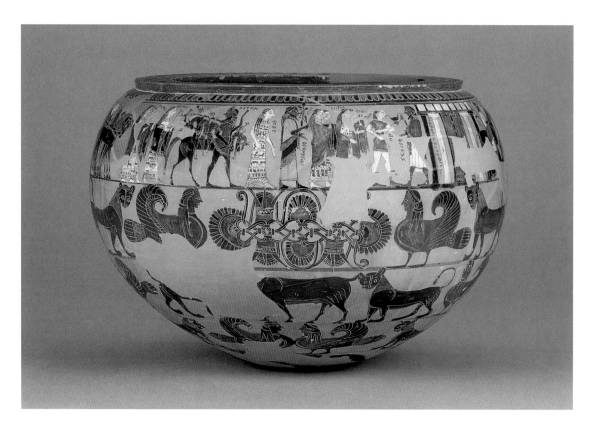

39 Sophilos dinos: Peleus welcomes the gods to his marriage feast. Made in Athens, 580 BC. Ht of bowl 28.0 cm. GR 1971.11–1.1

Sophilos developed a lively but unsophisticated style which was continued in the second quarter of the sixth century by a group of artists who, although they also produced a few dinoi and kraters, specialized in a particular type of ovoid neck-amphora. Almost all of these amphorai have been found in Italy, especially in the cemeteries of the Etruscans (the Tyrrhenoi, as the Greeks called them) at Vulci and Cerveteri, hence their name Tyrrhenian amphorai. It is very likely that these vases formed part of a deliberate export drive by the Athenians, for they seem to have filled a gap in the repertoire of Corinthian vases, which had previously been preferred by the Etruscans. The decorative scheme of these vases follows on from Sophilos' dinos: figured scene above, animal friezes below. The subject of the figured scene on fig. 40 is taken from the stories surrounding the war against Troy and the participants are again labelled – it is the sacrifice of Polyxena at the tomb of Achilles. Three Greek warriors, Amphilochos, Antiphates and Aias Iliades (the lesser Ajax), hold the rigid figure of Polyxena over the mound of Achilles' tomb, while Neoptolemos drives his sword into her throat. Diomedes is the warrior to the left, while the old men at either extremity are Nestor

40 *Tyrrhenian amphora showing the sacrifice of Polyxena; from Italy. Made in Athens, 570–560 BC; attributed to the Timiades Painter. Ht 39 cm. GR 1897.7–27.2*

Pylios (of Pylos) and Phoinix, who turns his back on the scene, perhaps in sorrow and shame.

The Corinthians, in their turn, sought to compete with Athens and in the 560s even began to coat their vessels with an orangey-red slip in imitation of the richer colour of Athenian clay. A fine jug (oinochoe) shows a duel flanked by the warriors' squires who patiently hold their masters' horses as they sit astride their own steeds (fig. 41). The painter has tried to name the heroes, but the letters do not make sense, enthusiasm perhaps outstripping knowledge. Another technical feature might be noted: the white is laid directly on the clay surface and outlined. This technique is typical of Corinthian work, but rare at Athens; indeed, Sophilos was one of the few Athenian artists to employ it, suggesting perhaps that he might have been trained at Corinth. His successors, such as the Timiades Painter who produced the sacrifice of Polyxena, placed the white on top of an initial layer of black slip in the regular Athenian fashion.

The oinochoe is the work of one of the last of the recognizable Corinthian artists, the Tydeus Painter. Thereafter, Corinthian vase-painting declined into the mundane or trivial. At Athens, however, the advent of the tyrant Peisistratos and his family brought many foreign contacts and considerable prosperity. We may observe something like a doubling in the number of vase-painters at work and at the same time the disappearance of the rural groups of painters, as Athens fast became a great urban centre. Athenian pottery also now gained domination over all the markets Corinth had previously won. It travelled west, to be buried in Etruscan tombs in Italy, on to France and even as far as Spain; it was exported east, deep into Anatolia and up into the Black Sea, and south to Egypt and Africa; and it even traversed the Alps. It was prized everywhere and by everybody.

Ancient sources record that in 566 BC the festival of Athena was enlarged, thus making a Greater Panathenaic Festival with competitions, including athletics and music, every fourth year and a Lesser Festival each intervening year. It also seems that this was when the custom of presenting special amphorai filled with specially produced Athenian olive oil to the victors was instituted (fig. 42). These

41 *Late Corinthian oinochoe showing a fight; on the rim are snakes. Made in Corinth, about 560 BC; attributed to the Tydeus Painter. Ht 23 cm. BM Cat. Vases B 39*

42 *Panathenaic prize-amphora, Athena; from Athens. Made in Athens, about 560 BC; attributed to the Burgon Group. Ht 61.5 cm. BM Cat. Vases B 130*

vessels bore on one side a representation of the event in which the winner was victorious, on the other a representation of Athena herself. On the example seen here is written on the left of Athena 'I am one of the prizes from Athens'. Athena's face, arms and feet were originally painted in white over the black, but the added colour has unfortunately flaked off, as has the white dolphin which once decorated her shield. This example is probably one of the earliest Panathenaic prize-amphorai to survive and may well date to the festival of 562 or 558 BC: it was found in a tomb near the northern gate of ancient Athens (the Acharnian Gate), where it had served as the ash urn, perhaps of a

Panathenaic victor. Such Panathenaic prize-amphorai were clearly needed in considerable numbers – more than 1400 and perhaps as many as 2000 every fourth year. Evidence from later centuries suggests that the officials responsible for the organization of the games let contracts to specific workshops.

From shortly before the middle of the sixth century comes the vase-painter Lydos, the first whose name is clearly foreign. An early work bears the signature *ho ludos egrsen* – this reveals that not only was he called 'the Lydian' but also, perhaps, that his knowledge of Greek was less than perfect, for he has written *egrsen* instead of *egraphsen*. Lydos' name and writing remind us of the welcome offered by Athens to foreign craftsmen from the beginning of the sixth century and of the other potters and painters whose names suggest foreign birth, including Skythes (Scythia), Kolchos (Kolchis), Mus (Mysia), Sikellos (Sicily), Thrax (Thrace) and Syriskos (Syria). Some of these craftsmen may have been what the Athenians called *metoikoi* (foreign residents), but others may have been slaves, for the ancient geographer, Strabo, tells us that the Athenians used to name their slaves after the peoples from whom they were imported. Although it is possible, therefore, that Lydos was a slave, something approaching certainty only comes with the case of a later and less talented black-figure painter who signed Lydos *egraphsen doulos ōn* (Lydos painted being a slave).

The earlier, and greater, Lydos decorated a variety of shapes including dinoi and neck-amphorai, which, like his bold style, link him back through the Tyrrhenian amphorai to Sophilos. One vase, however, looks like an amphora but is really much more (fig. 43). The potter has made a vessel within a vessel – the normal inner chamber accessible through the top, the invisible outer chamber through a round spout in the side and a hole in the base (stoppered when the vase was in use). This sort of vessel (a psykter-amphora) was used for cooling wine: the cold water was poured into the outer chamber, the wine into the inner. The scene on the front of this vase emphasizes its function: Dionysos stands to the right of the spout, drinking horn in hand. A maenad and three satyrs accompany the god of wine, while under the spout a young, hairless satyr plays with a hare. Dionysos' cloak shows a new feature – a zigzag fold. The gradual development of an understanding of drapery folds goes hand in hand with an increasing perception of the way the human body is constructed; both help us to chart the course of Greek vase-painting.

43 Opposite *Psykter-amphora attributed to the painter Lydos, showing Dionysos with satyrs and maenads. Made in Athens, about 550 BC. Ht 40.2 cm. BM Cat. Vases B 148*

The middle of the sixth century BC produced a number of excellent black-figure artists in Athens. One of these is known as the Amasis Painter, so called after the brilliant potter with whom he regularly collaborated. He produced a series of large amphorai and, most probably, the psykter-amphora decorated by Lydos (fig. 43), as well as small vases, like the round-mouthed jug (olpe) illustrated in fig. 44, which bears his signature as potter ('Amasis mepoiesen' – 'Amasis potted me'). The scene shows the decapitation of the Gorgon, Medusa. Perseus stands on the left turning his head away lest he be turned to stone, as he thrusts his sword deep into the monster's neck. On the far right stands Hermes, man's guide in life and death. The painting of this piece has a real delicacy and precision, very different from the rough immediacy of the followers of Sophilos. Indeed, the painter belongs closer to a tradition that depends on the work of Kleitias, whose masterpiece, the so-called François vase in Florence, is covered in a wealth of elegant miniature-painting. The Amasis Painter, however, is something more than a miniaturist: his style has strength as well as delicacy, breadth as well as precision. On this olpe the black-figure technique is fast reaching its acme: brushwork and incision are superbly controlled, while the beautifully balanced composition is typical of the painter's sense of form and structure.

We do not know the name of this painter for certain, but it is quite possible that potter and painter were the same man. The name Amasis is a hellenized form of the Egyptian name A-ahmes, which might suggest that Amasis was at least partly Egyptian, but there seems to have been a fashion among rich

44 *Olpe potted by Amasis and attributed to the Amasis Painter: Perseus kills the Gorgon Medusa. Made in Athens, about 550 BC. Ht 26 cm. BM Cat. Vases B 471*

Athenians for naming their sons after famous foreigners. Furthermore, we know that Amasis' son was called Kleophrades, a pure Greek name. This Kleophrades was also a potter, active at the end of the sixth century so that Amasis was either a Greek or a metic who secured citizenship. Such families of potters passing their craft from father to son, were probably the norm, and there is evidence for others.

The other great artist to appear around the middle of the sixth century was perhaps the finest of all painters to use the black-figure technique. His name, Exekias, is known from several signatures, both as potter and as painter. His painting combines the monumentality of Lydos with the delicacy of the Kleitian tradition. He was a master of speaking contour and form, as well as of incision. His potting is wonderfully crisp and sure and he seems to have been the first to attempt some new and improved shapes, including the calyx-krater and new forms of cup and amphora. He also may have been the first to use a new and difficult slip, so-called coral red or intentional red, which was achieved by mixing black slip with red ochre (cf. fig. 52 c) – the red ochre made the slip porous enough to re-admit oxygen in the final phase of firing, but yet the presence of black slip gave it a fine polished finish.

The British Museum has a splendid neck-amphora signed by Exekias as potter (fig. 45 and frontispiece). The painting is his, too. In a basically square but curving field he has created a bold triangle. Achilles, the hero of Troy, thrusts down with his spear into the throat of Penthesilea, queen of the Amazons. She has sunk to the ground as blood gushes from her throat. Their eyes seem locked together in this last moment of violence, but also perhaps the first moment of something more. Exekias achieves this sort of psychologically potent moment on a number of his other vases, and one need not perhaps dismiss as the creation of a later and more melodramatic age the story that Achilles fell in love with Penthesilea at the very instant in which he killed her.

In addition to the names of the two protagonists and the signature of Exekias, on the right of the group are the words 'Onetorides kalos' ('Onetorides is beautiful'). This idea of praising someone's beauty, both male and female (but male more frequently), begins around the middle of the sixth century and lasts through into the second half of the fifth. The intention seems to be to praise the favourite youth or courtesan of the moment. These golden boys of the Athenian upper class, however, like courtesans, came and went and one can trace their ever-changing parade from the vases. For at one moment a youth like Onetorides will

45 *Neck-amphora signed by Exekias as potter, and attributed to him as painter, showing Achilles killing Penthesilea; from Vulci. Made in Athens, 540–530 BC. Ht 41.6 cm. BM Cat. Vases B 210*

be praised by a number of painters, but after a while his name will be replaced by another's. These names, however, do sometimes also appear in the historical record, as with a favourite at the end of the sixth century, Leagros, who lived in the area of the Kerameikos and in later life became a general, or Euaion the son of the tragedian Aeschylus.

We wonder at this vase's remarkable figured scene, at the brilliance of Exekias' incised markings on armour, animal skin and cloth, at the delicate restraint of the added colours, at the calligraphy of the inscriptions and at the unerring precision of the subsidiary decoration. But Exekias signed as potter and our last word should perhaps be about the vase itself. The body is so finely potted and the contours so tight that it almost seems as if touching the vase might cause it to gently lift off like a balloon. The added elements, foot, handles and neck, all have the same clarity and perfection, while the careful preparation of the surface (Exekias must have given it a very fine wash of ochre to enhance its colour) and of the black slip have given him the perfect basis for what is truly a masterpiece of potting as well as painting.

Alongside Amasis and Exekias stands the series of so-called Little Master cups that grew out of the potter Ergotimos' work (he potted Kleitias' great krater – the François vase). Their potting is superb and they carry not only miniature painting (fig. 3) but also a plethora of inscriptions, including signatures (fig. 46) and lively exhortations to drink and be merry, which can become a form of decoration in their own right. There are some twenty-eight signatures of potters and only four of painters, a fact which, when it is combined with the frequently reduced level of decoration, seems to suggest that the potters were the leading figures in the group. The signatures reveal not only foreign ethnics, possible slave names, and a pair of brothers, but also the way that the craft of potting was passed from father to son and even, in one case, on to a grandson.

With excellence came experiment, both in painting and potting. We have noted how Exekias tried the effect on some of his vases of a coral-red slip, but other artists, like the Amasis Painter and some of the painters of the Little Master cups, employed more outline work than usual, often replacing the added white customary for female flesh with simple outlining. The rivalry between two excellent potters, Nikosthenes and Andokides, is neatly shown by two unusual vases decorated in the regular black-figure technique: one is a volute-handled krater, the other a neck-amphora (fig. 47). Both are exceptional in shape,

46 Cup signed by Tleson son of Nearchos as potter; from Kamiros (Rhodes). Made in Athens, about 540 BC. Ht 16.5 cm. BM Cat. Vases B 411

probably being derived directly from metal prototypes, both have their figured decoration confined to the neck and both bear the signature of their potter on the top of the rim.

Nikosthenes, who signed the volute-handled krater (fig. 47, left), was a particularly inventive potter with an exceptional eye for what would sell in the profitable market of Etruria. Two of the shapes he developed for this outlet were a special form of neck-amphora and a wine-dipper (kyathos), both imitating a local form made in the all black bucchero technique typical of Etruscan pottery (fig. 48). The kyathos also reveals a new Athenian technique of painting, one which left most of the vase black, perhaps the more to imitate the Etruscan original. This new technique, called the Six technique after Jan Six who first studied it, is really an extension of that used for the white flesh of women to include the whole decoration. The complete figure is now rendered in thickly applied whitish clay slip, inner details being marked with incision or added red. On this example the figured scene is kept to a minimum – Dionysos, seated on a stool, a heavily laden vine branch in one hand.

The Six technique has a certain freshness, but it does not seem really to have caught on and is soon confined to just a few shapes with ritual or funerary functions, such as phialai (bowls) and lekythoi (oil

47 (a) *Volute-krater signed by Nikosthenes as potter, showing scenes from a fight; from Italy. Made in Athens, 530–520 BC. Ht 37.5 cm. BM Cat. Vases B 364*

(b) *Neck-amphora signed by Andokides as potter and attributed to the painter Psiax; from Vulci. The scene on the neck shows Dionysos and satyrs. Made in Athens, 530–520 BC. Ht 39.5 cm. GR 1980.10–29.1*

48 Opposite, clockwise from front left (a) *Six-technique kyathos, showing Dionysos; from Italy. Made in Athens, 530–520 BC. Ht 13.8 cm. BM Cat. Vases B 693*

(b) *Etruscan bucchero neck-amphora. Made in Etruria, 570–520 BC. Ht 33.6 cm. GR 1984.10–23.1*

(c) *Black-figured neck-amphora signed on the rim by Nikosthenes as potter; from Italy. Made in Athens, 530–520 BC. Ht 33.4 cm. BM Cat. Vases B 296*

(d) *Etruscan bucchero kyathos. Made in Etruria in the sixth century BC. Ht 19.8 cm. BM Cat. Vases H 222*

bottles). Nikosthenes' other new technique, however, was to prove much more lasting and much more important for the future of vase-painting. This is the idea of painting on a white slip which was applied to the whole vase, an idea probably borrowed from the eastern Greek cities on the coast of Asia Minor where the technique was particularly common (fig. 52 d). Nikosthenes seems, indeed, to have borrowed much from the East, including some shapes. The phiale, a shallow bowl for pouring libations, is one of these, and the British Museum has a unique example with a white slip on the interior (fig. 49). This piece, like the kyathos discussed above, is not signed by Nikosthenes as potter, but the shape and manner of decoration suggest that it is from his workshop. The drawing, which is done in the black-figure technique, the width of the incisions being slightly enlarged to make them look more like the reserved markings on contemporary and earlier East Greek products, depicts in an inner frieze a hare-hunt and beyond, in an outer zone, a menagerie of foxes, partridge-like birds, snakes and a scorpion fancifully playing the pipes.

49 White-ground phiale decorated with a hare-hunt and animals; said to be from Capua. Made in Athens, about 520 BC. Diam. 21.7 cm. BM Cat. Vases B 678

At a number of moments in the sixth century glimpses of contact, in both directions, between the eastern Mediterranean and Athens can be seen, for not only do we find in Athens two painters called Lydos and borrowed East Greek decorative motifs and shapes, but we also find East Greek painters imitating Athenian work. Furthermore, it seems that there were important connections between some Greek cities and Italy that went beyond normal trading contacts. For, from shortly before the middle of the sixth century a succession of black-figure workshops were set up in central Italy. One appears to have mainland Greek origins, as is shown by a small hydria (fig. 50, left) that stands at the head of a series of black-figure vases made in Etruria (the misnamed 'Pontic' class). Other Etruscan groups seem to show East Greek influence, which has

50 (a) *'Pontic' hydria with youth on horseback between draped youths; attributed to the Eyre Painter. Made in Etruria, about 550 BC. Ht 26 cm. GR 1998.1–14.1*

(b) *Laconian cup with hero on horseback; attributed to the Rider Painter. Made in Laconia, 550– 540 BC. Diam. 17.7 cm. BM Cat. Vases B 1*

been thought to indicate that increasing pressure on the East Greek world, first from the Lydian empire and then from the rise of the Persians, caused East Greek craftsmen to emigrate to Italy. It is becoming clear, however, that potters were actually very mobile.

There were a number of other local schools in South Italy. The most important is known as 'Chalcidian' and was perhaps based at the Chalcidian Greek colony of Rhegion (modern Reggio) in the south, as is suggested by the script found on its products, a script which appears to be closest to that of Chalkis on Euboea. At its best, this school's products are majestic and very distinctive, but the potters were not above also looking east across the Mediterranean, as one of their more minor products, a small black-figure scent pot, known as a lydion, suggests (fig. 51,

51 (a) *East Greek ribbed lydion; from Gela in Sicily. Made in an East Greek centre, 550–500 BC. Ht 12.2 cm. GR 1863.7–28.91*

(b) *Chalcidian lydion decorated with animals. Made at Rhegion (?) in South Italy, 540–530 BC. Ht 7.6 cm. GR 1990.4–12.1*

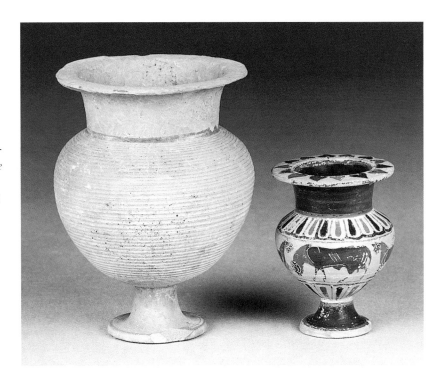

right). This shape is known in native Lydian pottery and, with ridges, in Lydian silver ware. The ridged example illustrated next to the Chalcidian version is of East Greek manufacture, although found at Gela on Sicily, and clearly echoes Lydian metal examples (fig. 51, left). On Sicily itself there was a minor school that produced small neck-amphorai, the so-called Megara Hyblaea Class, with its pale clay and red wash, a workshop that had strong connections with Chalcidian pottery.

There were, of course, other sixth-century schools of black-figure pottery on mainland Greece itself. That based in Laconia was one of the finest, with its thick white slip and unusual scenes (fig. 50, right). Like Athenian pottery, it was widely exported, reaching not only Italy (both Etruria and Taras, Sparta's daughter colony), but also Cyrenaica, Egypt and the eastern Greek world. Other schools, however, were of lesser quality and seemingly less in demand abroad, for example those in Boeotia and on Euboea, which depended on Athenian style, and the several centres in East Greece, where some craftsmen looked to Corinth and others to Athens or even Laconia.

6 ATHENS AS THE LEADER OF ALL GREECE

THE RED-FIGURE TECHNIQUE

Around 530 BC a new technique was invented in Athens that was to revolutionize Greek pottery. This was the 'red-figure' technique. It is the reverse of the black-figure scheme with its black figures on a red ground, for it has red figures against a black ground. It is important to realize, however, that these red figures are not achieved by painting with a red colour, but rather by painting the background and leaving the figures reserved in the natural orangey-red colour. We do not know who invented this technique, although Nikosthenes' interest in new ideas, the fact that some of the earliest examples of the new technique are to be found on unusual shapes, and the similarity in effect between the Six technique and the red-figure technique all make one wonder if he was its inventor. A small fragment of a cup found at Naukratis in Egypt illustrates this possibility, while showing how the new technique looked in its early stages (fig. 52 a). The fragment is, in fact, from a cup of the same shape as that potted by Tleson son of Nearchos (fig. 46), only the figured scene is, exceptionally, on the inside of the lip. The scene is taken from a feast or symposium – a figure reclines, phiale in hand, a cloak round his waist and legs and a cushion under his arm. The drawing is very simple and the technique clearly in its infancy.

The name, however, that most modern scholars associate with the inception of the red-figure technique is Nikosthenes' rival, Andokides. Andokides is known from a famous metrical inscription on a marble pillar, the base for a bronze statue dedicated on the Acropolis, that reads *[M]nesiades kerameus me kai Andokides anetheken* – Mnesiades the potter and Andokides dedicated me (the word potter appears only once for metrical reasons). Andokides' partner in this inscription is also known from his signature on a fragment of a large and unusual black-figure hydria (water jar), most probably from Saqqara in Egypt (fig. 52 b). It is possible that the joint dedication on the Acropolis was made on the occasion of the transfer of the ownership or direction of the business from the senior Mnesiades to the junior Andokides.

Andokides must have been a very successful potter, although he was perhaps less inventive than Nikosthenes – his only original shape is the special amphora with handles reaching to the rim, which he proudly signed (fig. 47, left). He was, however, more discriminating in the choice of his painters. The neck of the amphora was decorated by Psiax, a particularly adaptable painter who has left us works like this in a superb miniature black-figured style, as well as pieces employing coral red, white ground, Six technique and red-figure. If any painter had a hand

52 Clockwise from left (a) *Fragment from the lip of a cup showing a youth reclining at a banquet; from Naukratis. Made in Athens, 530–520 BC. Ht 7.3 cm. BM Cat. Vases E 134,2*

(b) *Fragment of the shoulder of a black-figured hydria; probably from Saqqara. Made in Athens, about 550 BC; signed by Mnesiades as potter. Width 11.0 cm. On loan from Dr Herbert A. Cahn, Basel (no. 859).*

(c) *Fragment of a red-figured cup with the head of a warrior stringing his bow; the area beyond the tondo has been given a slip of coral red. Made in Athens, 520–510 BC; signed by the potter Chachrylion. GR 1897.10–28.2*

(d) *Fragment of a white-slipped Chiot kantharos with a painted dedication; from Naukratis. Made on Chios, 570–550 BC. GR 1924.12–1. 755 and 808*

in the development of the red-figure technique, Psiax would be a good candidate.

Andokides also used an anonymous artist whom we call the Andokides Painter. In his hands the red-figure technique achieved stability and began to show its real potential: lines painted with a brush are inevitably more fluid than incised lines, however carefully executed, and now all interior markings on figures could be done in just this way. In addition, the black background seems to make the more naturally coloured figures stand out in three dimensions.

A number of vases of this period are sometimes called 'bilinguals', for on one side they are decorated in the old black-figure technique, on the other in the new red-figure scheme. Both Andokides and Nikosthenes produced such pieces. A detail from the red-figured side of a bilingual amphora decorated by the Andokides Painter (his partner, the Lysippides Painter, was responsible for the black-figured side) shows Herakles wrestling with the lion that terrorized the area around Nemea near Corinth (fig. 53). The red-figure technique has been improved since the cup fragment, for the painter here marks the contours of his figures with a bold, three-dimensional line nowadays called a 'relief line' (see p. 14). This line seems to have been achieved by using a much thicker mixture of slip than usual. In addition, the painter has also begun to experiment with the effect of thinning his slip to produce a light-brown colour. This thinned slip was eventually used to mark the numerous minor modulations of the body, such lines being called 'dilute glaze lines'. There are also, on this example, high-relief blobs to indicate curls on Herakles' head. Finally, added red is still employed, but much more sparingly than in the black-figure technique, for fillets around the hair and, here, for the lion's tongue.

Herakles was a very popular hero throughout the Greek world, but in Athens in the second half of the sixth century this popularity seems to have bordered on something of an obsession. John Boardman has suggested that this might reflect an interest taken by the Peisistratid tyrants in Herakles as a vehicle for propaganda, much as the Athenian democracy's interest in Theseus in the fifth century appears to have been politically motivated. Even if the hypothesis is as yet impossible to prove, the approach has the merit of encouraging the student of Greek vases to set them in their historical and political context. Indeed, the last quarter of the sixth century and the first quarter of the fifth were to see immense changes. In 528 BC the tyrant Peisistratos died and was suc-

53 *Detail from an*
amphora showing
Herakles wrestling with
the Nemean lion. Made
in Athens, about 520 BC;
attributed to the
Andokides Painter. Ht of
figured scene 18 cm. BM
Cat. Vases B 193

ceeded by his son Hippias, under whom the tyranny began to lose some
of its confidence. In 514 BC Hipparchos, Hippias' brother, was slain by
Harmodios and Aristogeiton and then, finally, in 510 BC the Peisistratid
tyranny fell and democracy began its slow birth. It was not long, however, before the Greeks came into conflict with the Persians in the east,
first on the coast of Asia Minor and then in Attica itself. In 490 BC they
defeated them at the battle of Marathon and then again in 480/479, but
only after the Persians had sacked the city of Athens itself.

   We turn now to a painter who was employed by both Andokides and
Nikosthenes, and that is Epiktetos. Epiktetos worked in black-figure
where his debt to his teacher Psiax is clearest, but his best work was
done in the new red-figure technique, especially on cups, some of
which are 'bilingual', and on plates (fig. 54). Two revellers fill the circular field of a signed plate; one plays the pipes, the other bends to lift a
large skyphos (deep cup) from the floor. The languid vertical of the

piper as he gently rocks forward onto his toes, the supply arched back of the man with one boot-clad foot balancing the heavy skyphos, together with the neat letters of Epiktetos' signature as painter, all combine to produce a superb composition. Beazley's comment on Epiktetos that 'you cannot draw better, you can only draw differently' is amply borne out by the flowing contours of these spare figures, their clear features and the smoothly rippled drapery over the man's back.

Alongside Epiktetos, who was completely at home with the red-figure technique, there emerged a group of experimenters, 'Pioneers' as they are usually called. One of these was Euphronios. His painting is technically excellent and superbly precise: he owes much to his teacher, again Psiax, as a detail from a very early work reveals, a cup signed by Chachrylion as potter (fig. 55). Later in his career Euphronios achieved a remarkable virtuosity, rendering every wrinkle

54 *Plate with two revellers. Made in Athens, 520–510 BC; signed by Epiktetos as painter. Diam. 18.8 cm. BM Cat. Vases E 137*

and knuckle and, one sometimes feels, every bone and sinew within, as if his figures were flayed anatomical specimens. His most spectacular work was done on the broad field of the calyx-krater, a shape which he decorated for the potter Euxitheos, and there he has left us a series of powerful mythological scenes that were to influence the works of contemporaries and pupils for several decades.

These Pioneers, so called because of their exploration of new complicated poses and views of the human figure, also included Phintias. On a water jar (hydria) signed by Phintias as painter we see youths fetching water from a lion's-head spout (fig. 56, left). The youth on the left is a fine study in strain, his elbows clamped tightly to his side as he holds his heavy hydria, while one of his fellows is distracted by a man behind him, causing him to twist right round, his left arm following the movement. There is much additional anatomical detail in dilute glaze, but this is really only visible on the vase itself. The drawing of water from the

55 Detail from a cup showing two warriors; from Vulci. Made in Athens, 520–510 BC; signed by Chachrylion as potter and attributed to the painter Euphronios. Ht of figures 8 cm. BM Cat. Vases E 41

fountain-house for domestic use was a woman's task in ancient Greece, so the youths here are probably to be thought of as supplying it for the *palaistra* (wrestling school), rather than for the symposium shown on the shoulder of the vase.

The Pioneers – Euphronios, Phintias, Euthymides, and a fewer lesser figures like Sosias, Smikros and Oltos – were clearly a close-knit group of artists. Sometimes they wrote challenges or greetings to each other on their vases and sometimes they even labelled their figures with each other's names. On some vases they have added other names against some of their figures and these names suggest a circle of friends that included musicians and hetairai. It is particularly interesting to notice one man, named Smikythos, who appears as the music teacher of Euthymides and as a musician on three other vases, in an athletic context and dining with his friends, for Smikythos was the name of the father of one of the most important vase-painters of the next generation, Onesimos, as a dedication from the Acropolis reveals, and Onesimos, moreover, worked in the workshop that the Pioneer, Euphronios, established.

Next to Phintias' red-figured hydria is a late black-figured piece produced by a member of a circle of artists, known as the Leagros Group (named after the youth praised on some of their vases and on some by the Pioneers), a group which endeavoured to compete with the Pioneers (fig. 56, right). The scenes on their vases are often violent in theme and heavy with complicated black masses. Here, two quarrelling heroes are only pulled apart with difficulty; their legs and arms restlessly criss-crossing the surface. The effect is powerful and dramatic, but the painters could not compete with the flexibility of red-figure and the talent of its practitioners. Black-figured painting soon passed into the hands of minor painters of slight vases, until it eventually died out around the middle of the fifth century – the only viable exception being, as we shall see, the Panathenaic prize-amphora. Outside Athens the black-figure technique, which had been taken up in the sixth century in a number of regions, including Italy and the East Greek cities, as well as mainland Greece itself, similarly came to an end around the close of the sixth century BC or soon after. Apart from a few minor survivals, as at Corinth, it was only in Boeotia that a significant but bizarre tradition continued during the fifth century.

A number of the red-figure Pioneers tried their hand at potting as well as painting, perhaps as commercial success came, but it was

56 (a) *Hydria with youths collecting water at a fountain. Made in Athens, about 510 BC; signed by Phintias as painter. Ht 54.1 cm. BM Cat. Vases E 159*

(b) *Hydria showing two quarrelling heroes. Made in Athens, 510–500 BC; attributed to the Leagros Group. Ht 50.7 cm. BM Cat. Vases B 327*

Euphronios who seems to have had the greatest impact. Indeed, after working as a painter for a number of potters for some ten years from around 520 BC we can follow his signatures as a potter of drinking cups down to about 470 BC. This is a prodigious career and it is further marked by a sculptural dedication on the Athenian Acropolis. All that remains is three fragments of the carefully inscribed base, but they suggest that it was made as a tithe, a tenth of the profits for one year perhaps, by Euphronios to Athena Hygieia. The date is the early 470s and the occasion most probably after the safe return to Athens following the defeat of the Persians in 480/479 BC and the successful re-establishment of his no doubt devastated workshop in the Kerameikos.

One of Euphronios' first and finest pupils turned out to be Onesimos, the son of his friend the musician Smikythos. His very earliest works depend heavily on Euphronios' style, but there is from the beginning a fresher, more vital spirit at work. From the interior of one of his early cups comes a simple but intimate human scene: an ageing reveller is seated on a low stool, one hand gripping his knotted stick, the food-basket above his head and the lyre by one foot setting the time and the place – an evening's feast (fig. 57). Before him stands a hetaira (courtesan) who wears a fancy hairnet and a fine linen chiton, so fine, indeed,

57 Interior of a cup showing a reveller and a courtesan; from Vulci. Made in Athens, 500–490 BC; signed by Euphronios as potter and attributed to the painter Onesimos. Diam. of tondo 18.6 cm. BM Cat. Vases E 44

that it is transparent. Her hands are at the cord around her waist; she is holding up her chiton to the right length by keeping her wrists to her sides as she does up her girdle. He reaches out one hand towards her and his mouth opens as he perhaps tries to dissuade her from leaving so soon. The way his legs surround her suggests the possession that he longs to extend, but his furrowed brow and pleading gesture reveal the hopelessness of his case. There is, however, understanding and tenderness in the way her head bends down towards him and in the gentleness of her self-possession.

The frontal pose of the hetaira, the man's frontal lower leg and completely foreshortened upper leg are all ideas that have grown out of the experiments of the Pioneers. Euphronios himself signed this cup as potter on one handle. Several other important cup-painters of the early decades of the fifth century also began their career under Euphronios' eye, but some of them went on to work for other potters. One of these was Douris, who moved on to the establishment of a potter called Python. Douris was certainly a prolific painter, leaving us some 250 examples of his work. Like most of his fellow cup-painters, he did, however, paint a few other shapes. Indeed, the British Museum has a particularly fine psykter signed by Douris, a rare mushroom-shaped wine-cooler that replaced the multiple vessels seen around the middle of the sixth century, the new shape being perhaps an invention of Nikosthenes (fig. 58). It was filled with wine and set to float in a krater of ice-cold water. Douris' decoration spreads right around the body, and the subject chosen is directly relevant to the vase's function, for we see a troop of satyrs, the companions of Dionysos, aged as usual by their debauchery but still capable of cavorting wildly in a boisterous ballet. They dance, do handstands, and one performs a prodigious feat of balancing, made even more remarkable by the imminent addition of wine into the kantharos so proudly and precariously poised.

Douris' drawing is very elegant and controlled. His earlier works, like the psykter, have some fire as well as elegance, but his later vases tend to become more academic. The method of attributing vases to particular hands is based on, among other things, a close observation of every line that goes to make up the painting, for every line is personal to its painter, part of his own individual 'handwriting'. Two typical features of Douris' style can be seen clearly on the London satyrs: the W-shaped hip line and the small arc at the junction of the lines marking the lower boundary of the pectorals.

58 Opposite *Psykter decorated with cavorting satyrs; from Cerveteri. Made in Athens, 500–490 BC; signed by Douris as painter. Ht 28.7 cm. BM Cat. Vases E 768*

It is with Douris that we find the occurrence of what seem to be forged signatures. One of the painters whose early works were potted by Euphronios was the so-called Triptolemos Painter. He has stylistic connections both with Onesimos and with Douris, but he was also influenced by other painters and worked for a number of other potters. His mature style, however, comes closest to that of Douris and not only does he imitate Douris' patternwork as well as figurework, but on two cups he imitates Douris' writing and his signature. I cannot help suspecting that the Triptolemos Painter is actually teasing his elder colleague. The potters' quarter, the ancient Kerameikos, was a small but lively world, peopled with craftsmen who looked at each other's work, talked to each other and no doubt tried to sell their wares to the same people, traders and citizens.

Alongside these painters who essentially specialized in decorating cups, or perhaps we should think rather in terms of potters who specialized in fashioning cups, there were also painters and potters who concentrated on larger vessels. One of the finest painters of pots in the early fifth century is known as the Berlin Painter, so named by Beazley after a vase in that city. He was a pupil of the Pioneers, in particular of Phintias and Euthymides. A splendid neck-amphora with twisted handles gives us a good idea of his quality and style (fig. 59). In a sea of black glaze the painter has isolated, as if under a spotlight, the figure of an ageing reveller. He walks along, *barbiton* (long lyre) pressed against one hip, the fingers of his left hand at its strings, those of his right gripping a plectrum. A stick is slipped nonchalantly under his arm and a plain cloak surrounds his shoulders. His

59 *Neck-amphora decorated with an ageing reveller; from Vulci. Made in Athens, about 490 BC; attributed to the Berlin Painter. Ht 49.4 cm. BM Cat. Vases E 266*

head and body turn, his attention seeming to be caught by the sudden billowing of his cloak. His lithe body is strangely both tense and languid: his muscles and sinews are taut, but his downturned head and slightly flexed knees impart a sense of languorous grace. This effect is to be found in a number of the Berlin Painter's other figures.

In the case of the Berlin Painter there are a number of easily recognizable features to his style, such as the little triangle at the junction of the lower contours of the pectorals and the pincer-like form of the ankle-bone. Many other features and details combine to enable us to make an attribution to the Berlin Painter, including subsidiary ornament and overall conception. The Berlin Painter's special talent lay in his ability to build small, elegant details into a graceful, living whole and then set his figure or group in perfect harmony with the vessel he was decorating. Thus, in this case, the curve of the shoulder of the vessel seems to complement the bunching of the reveller's drapery, while the turn of his head echoes the change in direction of the surface.

The other great pot-painter of this period is known as the Kleophrades Painter. His name derives from the fact that early in his career he decorated a pair of very large cups for the potter Kleophrades, the son of Amasis. The Kleophrades Painter's figures contrast strongly with those of the Berlin Painter: they are massive, heavy-set and powerful, as can be seen on a stamnos (storage jar) showing Theseus killing the robber Prokrustes, one of the bandits he met and disposed of on his journey to Athens (fig. 60). Details of style also differ from those of the Berlin Painter. There are, for example, no triangle at the junction of the pectorals and no pincer-like ankle-bones; instead, we have a solid line continuing from the pectorals down the median line as far as the navel and simple L-shaped ankle-bones. Other characteristic features are the arc-like depression between

60 *Stamnos showing Theseus and Prokrustes. Made in Athens, 490–480 BC; attributed to the Kleophrades Painter. Ht 31.9 cm. BM Cat. Vases E 441*

Theseus' clavicles and his incised hair contour. This latter feature, in fact, belongs to the formative years of the red-figure technique, before the idea of leaving a reserved contour had been developed. The Kleophrades Painter's liking for it may reflect not a reactionary tendency but a desire to reduce the artificial boundary between hair and air to a minimum.

The Kleophrades Painter's teacher was the Pioneer, Euthymides, and one of the lessons that he, like the Berlin Painter, learnt was the device of the three-quarter view of the foot – used here on Prokrustes. The robber's three-quarter face, however, is a new development that we begin to see around 490 BC. Both devices are intended to add depth to a two-dimensional representation, as is the Kleophrades Painter's own idiosyncratic extension of the median line down from the pectorals to the navel. The double curve of this line turns it into a modelling line, thereby suggesting the fullness of chest and stomach. It is often assumed that such ideas were borrowed from free painting, whether on wall or panel. This is, of course, quite possible and indeed a number of such borrowings seem to have been made around the middle of the fifth century, as we shall see later, but it need not be true in the first quarter; indeed, one can actually observe some painters of this period experimenting with and developing such ideas and techniques for themselves.

The lines that mark out the interior form of the naked male body on red-figure vases are of two types. There are the strong, black 'relief' lines that trace the contour and the major inner forms and the softer, brown 'dilute glaze' lines that distinguish other muscular planes and patterns. It seems clear that vase-painters developed this system with the intention that it would best reflect the degrees of projection of the forms and muscles of the body – the major projections that resulted in deeper shadow being marked with the relief lines, the softer areas of shadow rendered in dilute glaze. This amounts to a system of tonal gradation and was, like the development of elaborate poses, a step on the path towards the portraying of the three-dimensionality of the human figure.

Alongside such red-figured vases we also find pieces decorated in outline over a white ground. The use of a white slip was, as has already been mentioned, developed around 530 BC. At first the decoration was done in the regular black-figure technique, but soon the effect of outline drawing was tried. This idea was quickly taken up, especially by artists now trained in the red-figure technique. Onesimos, Douris and the Triptolemos Painter all tried it, but one of the most successful and best preserved examples was painted by another cup-painter of the peri-

od whom we call the Brygos Painter after the potter for whom he usually worked. This example is not, however, on a cup but on a jug (see
back cover). Here we see the lone figure of a women spinning wool; she
uses a short distaff and a weighted spindle – a method still to be found
in isolated parts of Greece even today. She is a model of serious concentration, head slightly bent as she watches the thread. But who is she?
Is she a dedicated and virtuous housewife, or perhaps one of the Fates,
spinning the thread that carried man's destiny? We cannot know; indeed,
the very ambiguity of a scene is something on which Greek artists often
played.

The unusual technique and exceptional quality of this vase suggest
that it was designed as a special piece to be given as a gift or dedication.
It would indeed have made a very suitable gift for a woman on her wedding – an image to emulate – or for a woman on her death – a memo-
rial to what she had been. It is said to come from Locri in southern Italy
and its perfect preservation suggests that it may well have come from the
tomb of a Greek settler there. Greeks had, in fact, developed the coastal
districts of southern Italy to such an extent that the whole area later
came to be called Magna Graecia ('Great Greece').

From the northernmost part of the Greek sphere of influence in Italy,
from near Capua in Campania, comes a remarkably rich grave group.
The grave had been robbed in antiquity, its metal vessels and jewellery
probably stolen, but seven superb vases were left and they are currently
reunited in the British Museum (fig. 62). One of the finest of the vases,
the cup, is signed by Brygos as potter on the edge of the foot, and so the
tomb has been dubbed the 'Brygos Tomb'. This cup was decorated by
the Brygos Painter, like the white-ground jug with the spinster. The
tondo inside shows the warrior Chrysippos pouring a libation with the
aid of a girl called Zeuxo before leaving for battle, a quiet, moving scene
in contrast to the riot outside, where satyrs threaten the gods themselves. There, the queen of the gods is protected by Hermes and
Herakles from a slightly hesitant band of satyrs on one side (fig. 61), but
on the other side Iris has no such protectors and is quickly caught by a
more unbridled troop, egged on by Dionysos himself.

The decoration of the large skyphos signed by Hieron as potter, however, is much more sober. The painting is by Makron, another
cup-painter of the first quarter of the fifth century who, like Douris and
the Brygos Painter, was much influenced by Onesimos. Here we see an
important religious event, Triptolemos in his magical winged and

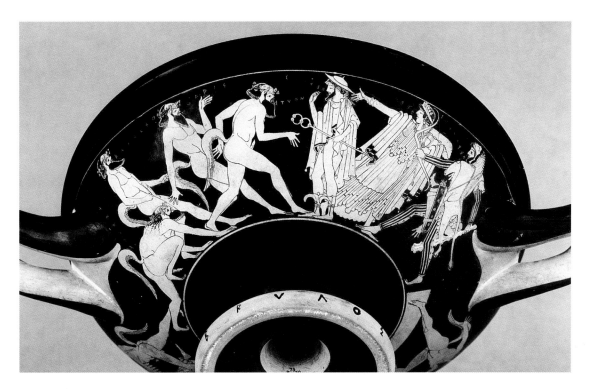

61 *Cup with satyrs attacking Hera; from Capua (Brygos Tomb). Made in Athens, about 490–480 BC; signed by the potter Brygos and attributed to the Brygos Painter. Diam. 27.6 cm. BM Cat. Vases E 65*

62 Overleaf, clockwise from front left *Pottery from the Brygos Tomb near Capua:*

(a) *Rhyton in the form of a sphinx with scenes showing Kekrops and his daughters. Made in Athens, 470–460 BC; attributed to the potter Sotades and the Sotades Painter. BM Cat. Vases E 788*

(b) *Stamnos showing Eos and Kephalos. Made in Athens, 470–460 BC; attributed to the Deepdene Painter. Karlsruhe B 1904*

(c) *Skyphos with Triptolemos about to take corn to mankind. Made in Athens, 490–480 BC; signed by Hieron as potter and attributed to the painter Makron. BM Cat. Vases E 140*

(d) *Stamnos showing Eos and Kephalos. Made in Athens, 470–460 BC; attributed to the Deepdene Painter. New York 1918.74.1 (Rogers Fund)*

(e) *Drinking vessel in the form of a sphinx vase depicting Eos and Tithonos (?). Made in Athens, 470–460 BC; attributed to the Tarquinia Painter. Ht 33.8 cm. BM Cat. Vases E 787*

(f) *Drinking vessel in the form of a ram's head. Made in Athens, 470–460 BC; attributed to the potter Sotades. BM Cat. Vases E 800*

(g) *Cup with Chrysippos and Zeuxo on the interior. Made in Athens, 490–480 BC; signed by Brygos as potter and attributed to the Brygos Painter. BM Cat. Vases E 65*

wheeled seat about to set off to bring corn to mankind. Persephone is on the right, helping in the farewell libation, while behind the chariot is Demeter, her mother. On the extreme right is the charming young figure of the nymph Eleusis, for it is at Eleusis that the event is taking place, and the torches held by Persephone and her mother are the typical paraphernalia of the Eleusinian Mysteries. Makron was particularly fond of elaborate drapery and his painting of Demeter's cloak recalls those worn by some of the goddesses on Sophilos' dinos (fig. 39), although there is a world of difference in the understanding of a garment's material and the way it hangs.

These two vases from the Brygos Tomb date around 490–480 BC, but the remaining pieces of the group date from after the Persian Wars, indeed to the decade 470–460 BC. It is likely that the two earlier pieces were prized possessions of the dead, whereas the later vases were bought especially for the burial. This idea is strengthened by the fact that two of the later vases are in the form of a sphinx, a guardian of the dead, and that there is a definite concentration in the figured scenes on abduction, a theme which was often associated with untimely death.

The two stamnoi (storage jars), which were not bought by the British Museum at the time of their discovery, but were sold later, one going to the Badisches Landesmuseum in Karlsruhe, the other to the Metropolitan Museum of Art in New York, are both by the same painter, the Deepdene Painter, and the same potter (perhaps called Oreibelos). The Deepdene Painter is a capable artist but his painting never rises above the purely decorative: scheme, movement and gestures all derive from earlier works, but the fire and passion are gone; drapery is more severe and less calligraphic. The same may be said of the painter of the rougher and less well preserved of the two sphinx vases (fig. 62 e), the Tarquinia Painter. He carried on the tradition of Onesimos and his followers within Euphronios' workshop and was chiefly a cup-painter, unlike the Deepdene Painter who specialized in larger vases, especially stamnoi.

The remaining two vases, the more elaborate sphinx vase (fig. 62 a) and the vase in the shape of a ram's head (fig. 62 f), are from the workshop of the potter Sotades. Sotades was an inventive potter who seems to have been particularly fond of vases with modelled parts. The interest shown in the fifth century for such vases is, as it was in the seventh, the result of contact with the East, in particular now with Persia. Sotades' sphinx is a true rhyton. Wine was poured into it, with the spout between the legs closed; the stopper, or more likely the finger, was then removed and the wine allowed to flow out, usually into a phiale or bowl, thereby aerating it and making it foamy. The Tarquinia Painter's sphinx, however, has no such hole and really belongs to the class of human or animal-headed drinking vessels, as does the Sotadean ram's head vase. Besides such fanciful creations, Sotades was also interested in the use of difficult techniques such as coral red, white ground and gilding. Like Nikosthenes before him, he succeeded in capturing a number of far-flung markets, for his vases reached not only Capua and elsewhere in Italy, but also Cyprus, the northern shores of the Black Sea, Memphis in Egypt and Meroë in distant Nubia, and even Persia itself, for pieces are known from both Susa and Babylon. In his painting, too, Sotades – for painter and potter are here most likely to be one and the same – endeavoured to match his subjects to his market. This fact raises the possibility that the deceased in the case of the Capua tomb was an Athenian and not the Etruscan he is usually thought to have been, since the red-figured decoration on the rim of our sphinx vase centres around purely Athenian figures – Kekrops, a legendary king of Athens, and his children. Furthermore, the Athenian connection seems to be maintained on the Deepdene Painter's two stamnoi, which both show, on one side, Eos chasing Kekrops' son, Kephalos, while the reverse of the Karlsruhe stamnos has yet another Athenian myth, Boreas carrying off Oreithyia, daughter of Erechtheus, a second legendary king of Athens.

The second quarter of the fifth century also witnessed the final flowering of Euphronios' cup workshop. One of the last painters that he employed is known as the Pistoxenos Painter who has left us some wonderful work on a white ground. A cup in the British Museum from Rhodes shows an image of Aphrodite, as the figure is labelled, gently floating through the bright air on the back of a goose, serene, beautiful and untouchable (fig. 63). It is the Pistoxenos Painter's last great masterpiece and is remarkable for the new, softened technique that used only dilute glaze lines for contours, for the purple red used on the cloak and even the borders of the patterned garment worn under it, and also for the way that the eye is now drawn properly in profile. In the sixth century the human eye was regularly drawn as if it was seen from the front and, although the Pioneer Sosias has left us an example of a fully understood profile eye, this naturalistic development did not find acceptance until the time of the Pistoxenos Painter's late work and that of his pupil the Penthesilea Painter. It was with the Penthesilea Painter that

63 White ground cup with Aphrodite on a goose; from Kamiros, Fikellura tomb 43 (Rhodes). Made in Athens, about 460 BC; attributed to the Pistoxenos Painter. Diam. 24.3 cm. BM Cat. Vases D 2

Euphronios' shop achieved a sudden, late expansion that saw frequent examples of painters sharing the decoration of a single cup. But, sadly, it soon became overstaffed and under-talented, ripe for the collapse that it suffered around the middle of the fifth century.

Another group of painters, Mannerists as they are called for their somewhat archaising manner, may best be represented by their finest scion, the Pan Painter, whose quirky charm regularly puts him above their normal level in terms of quality. On a large oinochoe (fig. 64) we see the wild and winged god of the north wind, Boreas, pursuing Oreithyia and her sister, the daughters of Erechtheus, the old king of Athens, who is shown seated and in despair. This theme seems to have gained a sudden popularity after the sea-battle off Cape Artemision, when the Athenians called on their 'father-in-law' Boreas to help them smash the Persian ships, as Herodotos tells us. The storm destroyed some 200 Persian ships and ultimately gave the Greeks their chance of victory at Salamis.

The Pan Painter worked on shapes both large and small, but another workshop concentrated on larger forms and achieved both Classical dignity and presence in its figures. On a monumental bell-shaped krater by one member, known as the Altamura Painter, the departure of two warriors is depicted (fig. 65). It is impossible to tell whether the scene is mythical or contemporary, but whatever the painter had in mind, the Athenian viewers of the scene must have thought of the Persian invasions and their own heroically stubborn defence of their city. Broad,

64 Oinochoe with Boreas chasing Oreithyia; from Vulci. Made in Athens, about 470 BC; attributed to the Pan Painter. Ht 35.3 cm. BM Cat. Vases E 512

65 *Bell-krater showing the departure of two warriors. Made in Athens, 470–460 BC; attributed to the Altamura Painter. Ht 40.5 cm. GR 1961.7–10.1*

plain surfaces and deliberate gestures have secured a real grandeur and a sense of determination.

It is in the workshop of the Altamura Painter and his follower, the Niobid Painter, that we first see, sometime in the 460s, a particularly important new development: the breaking up of the regular single ground level into a number of small, separate ground-lines spread up and down the surface of the vase in an attempt to add a feeling of space and depth to the picture. This scheme has been compared with the detailed account in Pausanias' *Description of Greece*, the second-century AD equivalent to the *Blue Guide*, of two works by the wall-painter Polygnotos of Thasos in a building at Delphi that also dated to the 460s BC. It has, therefore, been assumed that the idea was developed in the realm of wall-painting and was thence borrowed by vase-painters.

Few vase-painters of this period whole-heartedly adopted this new idea and it only began to be used with any regularity for seated figures in a landscape, as on a remarkable hydria with a scene from the story of Andromeda (fig. 66). King Kepheus of Ethiopia, in order to release his country from a sea-monster sent by Poseidon, who was offended by the *hubris* of the king's wife, was forced to offer his daughter, Andromeda, as a sacrifice to it. On the shoulder of the hydria, we see the distraught king seated on a mound on the right, forehead against his hands, as his Ethiopian servants prepare the holes for the two poles to which Andromeda will be tied. She is half carried to the spot, fainting perhaps with fear, while behind her comes a procession of figures with gifts as for a bride, for she will die before she can have a bride's dowry and so it must go with her to the grave.

On this vase father and daughter wear the elaborate oriental costume that is often associated with scenes from drama. It is very likely, therefore, this piece, together with a small group of vases of the same decade (450-440 BC), shows the influence of Sophokles' play, *Andromeda*. Such a connection is of particular interest, for Aristotle tells us that scene paintings first began to be used in the theatre with the works of Sophokles (i.e. from *c*.468 BC). The impact of both panel-painting and stage-painting on the more ambitious vase-painters of the mid fifth century must have been considerable. Indeed, once this trend for borrowing techniques and scenes from free-painting had begun, it perhaps spelled the end of vase-painters as important and independent artists, a status which they had increasingly enjoyed since the sixth century. For,

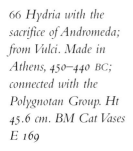

66 *Hydria with the sacrifice of Andromeda; from Vulci. Made in Athens, 450–440 BC; connected with the Polygnotan Group. Ht 45.6 cm. BM Cat Vases E 169*

from this time we start to see a decline in the number of painters' signatures (this was followed later by a similar decline in the number of potters' signatures), until all signatures died out early in the fourth century in Athens. Nevertheless, despite this downward turn, some vase-painters working on a white ground seem to have been able to adapt their technique more readily than those employing the ordinary red-figure scheme so that they at least could echo the new advances being made outside their own discipline.

The most important shape to be decorated with a white ground proved to be the lekythos. This shape, which had a long history in Greek pottery, was designed to hold sweet-smelling oil and was regularly associated with burials. It was, therefore, a suitable vessel to be given the fragile and probably expensive white slip. On the left of fig. 67 is a white-ground lekythos dating to around 460 BC, which is probably the work of the Villa Giulia Painter, a follower of the cup-painter Douris. The technique is the same as that used on the Pistoxenos Painter's Aphrodite cup, only a more colouristic effect has been sought by using two different shades of purplish red, one almost black, for the woman's drapery and a thick white to give her skin a different tone from that of the background.

This 'second' white for female flesh and the rather restricted purplish range of added colours, however, seem to have proved unpopular. Furthermore, the fact that these vases were now being used almost exclusively as offerings in the tomb, and so did not have to withstand any sort of wear, meant that the painters could begin to experiment with matt colours in a wider variety of shades that would not be so hard-wearing. The results must have been very beautiful, but all too often the added washes of colour have faded away, as on the fine piece on the right of fig. 67. This lady and her maid are the work of the Achilles Painter, an important artist who carried on the tradition of the Berlin Painter down to the time of the building of the Parthenon. His earliest white-ground lekythoi used the 'second' white of the Villa Giulia Painter's piece, but he soon abandoned it in favour of the experiments made by others. On this example the matt red of the lady's bundle of clothing is still quite well preserved and one can just make out on the original that its fold lines are yellow. The wash given to the garments worn by both women has, however, completely disappeared and we are left only with the sketchy contour lines, which give thus the misleading effect of absolutely transparent material. We can but guess at what colour

67 (a) *White-ground lekythos depicting a seated woman; from Gela. Made in Athens, about 460 BC; attributed to the Villa Giulia Painter. Ht 35.7 cm. BM Cat. Vases D 20*

(b) *White-ground lekythos with a woman and her maid; from Athens. Made in Athens, about 440 BC; attributed to the Achilles Painter. Ht 36.3 cm. BM Cat. Vases D 48*

the Achilles Painter actually used – it may have been a pale yellow-ochre or a grey-brown, both of which can be found on other of his works.

The Achilles Painter's women are imbued with the grace and confidence that one naturally attributes to the womenfolk of rich and powerful Periklean Athens – tall, serene and beautiful, like Olympian goddesses. But the potter of the day had no such romantic ideals. For the sake of his customer's pocket he has constructed within this beautiful gift to the dead a deceptively small false interior, thus turning a generously large lekythos into a miserly offering of oil.

The Achilles Painter, however, was also a master of both the black- and red-figure techniques, leaving us Panathenaic prize-amphorai and some of the best red-figure of the high Classical period. A fine neck-amphora may stand as an example (fig. 68). It isolates on one side a young rider, wearing a short cloak and a broad-rimmed traveller's hat hanging round his neck. This vase must date from just the period when the Parthenon and its elaborate sculptures were being planned. The horseman, thus, seems closely related to those on the frieze showing the Panathenaic procession, while the woman on the reverse might have stepped out of the parade of women on the east frieze.

A number of other vases of the third quarter of the fifth century and later do indeed reflect the Parthenon sculptures, pediments, metopes and frieze. This is hardly surprising, for it is difficult to underestimate the impact on the artistic community of Athens of the

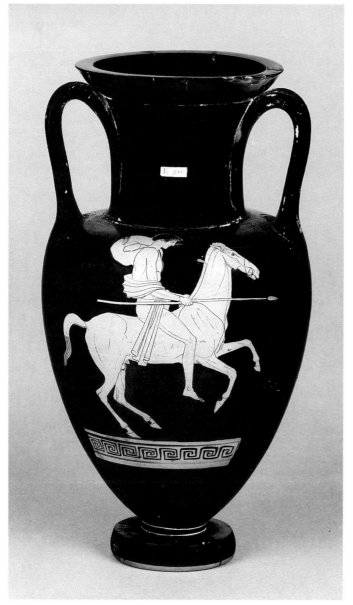

68 *Neck-amphora with a mounted youth. Made in Athens, 440–430 BC; attributed to the Achilles Painter. Ht 33 cm. BM Cat. Vases E 300*

69 *Stamnos with Herkales and the centaur Eurytion. Made in Athens, 440–430 BC; signed by Polygnotos as painter. Ht 40.5 cm. GR 1898.7–16.5*

great Periclean building programme, especially the intensity of work on the Parthenon itself (447/6-433/2 BC). Thus it is possible that a stamnos in the British Museum, signed by the vase-painter Polygnotos and showing Herakles rescuing the daughter of Dexamenos from the centaur Eurytion, also reflects elements of the south metopes that similarly showed scenes from the fight between the Greeks and the centaurs (fig. 69). The style of Polygnotos and his group derives from the Niobid Painter's circle and the tradition is carried on through some important artists of the latter part of the century and even into the fourth century. During Polygnotos' time it was an expanding workshop that produced chiefly large vases. We might imagine that his name was perhaps given him by his father, probably a member of the Niobid Painter's fellows, in honour of the great wall-painter from Thasos.

7

THE DIFFUSION OF
RED-FIGURE

If the middle decades of the fifth century were years of peace and great prosperity, dominated by Athens' rise under Perikles from leader of a league of Greeks against the Persians to ruler of an empire, ready to undertake grand building programmes, then the last quarter was a time of war. In 431 BC open conflict broke out between the super-powers, Athens and Sparta. This must have had a profound impact on Attica and the city, for the Spartans repeatedly invaded Attica and burnt the crops, forcing many of the country people to move into Athens or the space between the long walls that linked Athens to her port at the Piraeus. And in this overcrowded condition in 430 and 429 BC the plague struck, carrying off Perikles and tens of thousands of others. After some ten years of war there was an uneasy truce, the Peace of Nikias, which lasted until 415 when Athens thrust west in a desperate attempt to seize the riches of Syracuse. This attempt, spearheaded by the brilliant but reckless Alkibiades, was doomed to failure, and after a further ten years, in 404 BC, Athens surrendered to Sparta.

The 430s seem to have been years of change in the world of Greek pottery-making. The red-figure technique, of course, had been sporadically imitated in a number of parts of the Greek or at least Hellenised world since the second quarter of the fifth century – namely in Boeotia, in Etruria and Campania, and even on Lemnos. From the 430s we begin to find, however, the reinvigoration of some of these schools and the development of other new ones at Corinth, Elis, Sparta and Eretria, on Crete and in northeastern Greece (fig. 70), as well as, of course, in several parts of southern Italy and Sicily. Potters and painters, as we saw in the late eighth century, in the early seventh century and in the early sixth century, did sometimes migrate and this may be what happened in the last third of the fifth century, perhaps driven by a number of factors, including the deprivations in Athens, the threat of attack, and the dream of an easier life in the west. But it is equally possible that such conditions resulted in a drop in production in Athens, a decline in trade, and consequent attempts by local potters to supplement supply with their own creations.

70 (a) *Boeotian calyx-krater with a flying Nike; said to be from Euboea. Made in Boeotia, about 420 BC; attributed to the Painter of the Great Athens Kantharos. Ht 28 cm. GR 1910.4–18.1*

(b) *Chalcidic skyphos with Eros and a woman. Made in northeast Greece, 380–360 BC; attributed to the Painter of Olynthos 5.141. Ht 15 cm. GR 1955.4–18.1*

(c) *Elean pelike with a satyr and a maenad; from Cyrenaica. Made in Elis, about*

It is, of course, extremely difficult to chart such migrations, for it actually means recognizing a painter active in two centres. In one case, this does seem to be possible, for the Suessula Painter decorated not only pieces made of Athenian clay but also some of Corinthian clay. His story, however, is far from straightforward, for it has been suggested that a graffito on one of his works in Athenian clay might indicate that he was actually of Corinthian origin, an idea perhaps supported by his liking

71 *Column-krater with Apollo and Marsyas. Made in Athens, about 410 BC; attributed to the Suessula Painter. Ht 31.7 cm. BM Cat. Vases E 490*

for the column-krater, a shape very much out-of-fashion in Athens and known in antiquity as the Corinthian Krater (fig. 71). Nevertheless, other works indicate that, after a stay in Corinth, he must have journeyed back to Athens and ended his career there. As a result, one must take into account the possibility that potters and painters, at least by the latter part of the fifth century, could be very mobile, travelling to and fro between pottery-making centres.

The beginnings of the new school in Elis has sometimes been explained in terms of the presence of Athenian potters and painters in the retinue of Pheidias, when he created the great gold and ivory statue of Zeus in the temple at Olympia. Whatever its origin, by the early fourth century there seem to have been close connections with workshops in Apulia in South Italy. Indeed, it is possible that some artists even left Elis for *Megale Hellas*.

Of all these new schools, whether inspired by emigrant or visiting Athenian potters or by artists who were for a time trained there, it was really those that developed in southern Italy and on Sicily that were to have long and significant stories. It is often assumed that some of these artists had accompanied the Athenian settlement of Thurii in 443 BC, but there is, as yet, no archaeological evidence to support this plausible theory. The earliest recognized artist is the Pisticci Painter, and he seems to have begun his career in the 430s, although his style owes something to Athenian painters of the middle of the century, including the Achilles Painter and the Polygnotan Group. It is interesting to note, therefore, that some of these Athenian artists produced imitations of native One of these pieces was found near Bari on the Adriatic coast of Apulia (perhaps all were), where there appears to be evidence for the activity of immigrant Athenian potters.

A bell-shaped krater with an Eros chasing a youth, a standard work by the Pisticci Painter, may be compared with a similar scene on a small contemporary Athenian pelike (storage jar) by a minor artist known as the Hasselmann Painter, which was found in Italy (fig. 72). The difference in style and treatment, however, is quite noticeable: in

72 (a) Bell-krater with Eros and a youth. Made in Lucania, 440–430 BC; attributed to the Pisticci Painter. Ht 23.9 cm. BM Cat. Vases F 39

(b) Pelike with Eros and a youth. Made in Athens, 440–430 BC; attributed to the Hasselmann Painter. Ht 21 cm. BM Cat. Vases E 397

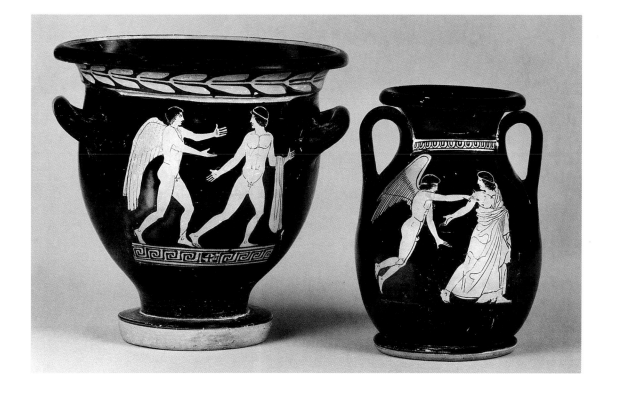

the colonial version the Eros is earthbound and rigid and the youth's drapery is heavy and towel-like, while on the Athenian vase there is still a sprightly charm to the Eros and the youth's himation looks, in comparison, far more like real, warm material. Although there is much that is Attic about the Pisticci Painter's work, there is also much that is radically different, so that we may not be witnessing in him the first of any migrants, but perhaps one of the first of their pupils. Nevertheless, the Pisticci Painter demonstrates a remarkable knowledge of Athenian pottery, even producing a black-figured Panathenaic amphora complete with prize inscription, which imitates those produced by the Achilles Painter, although it gives itself away in details of both style and shape.

Simple subjects and rather stiff drawing are typical of the earliest products of these South Italian vase-painters. Quite rapidly, however, the artists became more independent and adventurous. On a much more

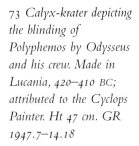

73 *Calyx-krater depicting the blinding of Polyphemos by Odysseus and his crew. Made in Lucania, 420–410 BC; attributed to the Cyclops Painter. Ht 47 cm. GR 1947.7–14.18*

ambitious calyx-shaped krater dating from about 415–410 BC we see Odysseus and his companions set about blinding the one-eyed Cyclops, Polyphemos, as he lies in a drunken stupor in his dark cave (fig. 73). The multi-level scheme ultimately derives, of course, from the ideas of the mainland wall- and panel-painters of the mid-fifth century BC, but whether it was through the medium of Polygnotan vase-painters or even stage-painters we cannot know. In this case, however, the presence of two frolicking satyrs on the right suggests that the subject of the scene is dependent in some way on a satyr play, perhaps Euripides' *Cyclops*, which was probably first produced in Athens around the time that this vase was made.

A group of potters' kilns at Metapontion (modern Metaponto) was found to contain fragments of vases by the most important pupil of the Pisticci and Cyclops Painters, the Amykos Painter, as well as large quantities of broken vases and kiln wasters by his immediate followers. This evidence, together with the number of finds from the surrounding area of the Pisticci Painter's own work, suggests that his school moved across the peninsula to Metaponto. We shall notice later, however, that these South Italian painters were quite mobile: indeed, by the beginning of the fourth century, one of the Amykos Painter's followers seems to have moved as far north as Etruria.

Some time around 430–420 BC a second workshop arose, based perhaps at Taras (modern Taranto). The first major artist of this group is called the Sisyphus Painter. He painted some vases in a simple, plain manner, rather like those of the Pisticci Painter and his followers, but he also decorated other rather grander pieces, perhaps under the influence of monumental works imported from Athens. A particularly fine krater with volute-shaped handles gives us a good idea of the Sisyphus Painter's best (fig. 74). The multi-levelled fight between Greeks and Amazons includes an ambitious dead figure in the foreground. We know of an important wall-painting in the Stoa Poikile at Athens by Mikon that had this theme and it seems quite possible that its influence was still being felt in the later fifth century, even in South Italy.

Around the time of the Athenian expedition to Syracuse in 415 BC the first red-figure vases appear to have begun to be made on Sicily and the two events may not be wholly unrelated, for this period must have seen a radical diminution in the amount of pottery imported from Athens. The first recognizable artist is the so-called Chequer Painter, named after his favoured border and cushion pattern (fig. 75); his style

74 Opposite *Volute-krater with Greeks fighting Amazons; from Ruvo. Made in Apulia, 410–400 BC; attributed to the Sisyphus Painter. Ht 66.9 cm. BM Cat. Vases F 158*

75 Right *Calyx-krater showing a symposium and the game of kottabos. Made on Sicily, 410–400 BC; attributed to the Chequer Painter. Ht 36 cm (foot restored). BM Cat Vases F 37*

recalls the later followers of Polygnotos. The scene shows a man and a youth at a symposium, as they play the game of *kottabos*. The bearded man, having called out the name of his lover or would-be lover, has just flicked the dregs of wine in the bottom of his cup at a special target, a small disc on top of a pole, which when dislodged would clang against the large disc half way down the pole. Eros hovers on the left, holding a garland, ready to crown him if he is successful and thus mark out his success in love. This game was actually of Sicilian origin, but it was played throughout the Greek world and in Aristophanes' *Acharnians* Dikaiopolis even suggests that a too serious game of it led to the Peloponnesian War!

Alongside the grand style of the Polygnotans of the years after the middle of the fifth century, a style that we have seen had a great impact on the South Italian schools, there had developed at Athens a prettier manner, usually reserved for smaller pot shapes and cups. This culminated in the last two decades of the century in the work of the Meidias Painter and his followers. The most celebrated work from this group is a large hydria in the British Museum which bears the signature of the potter Meidias (fig. 76). It was the pride of Sir William Hamilton's collection, acquired by the British Museum in 1772, the Museum's founding collection of Greek vases. The body of the vase is divided into two separate zones by an ornamental border. The lower zone depicts Herakles in the garden of the Hesperides – the Hesperides ('daughters of evening'), together with a dragon, guarded a wonderful tree on which grew golden apples, the target of Herakles' final labour. The key section shows three of the Hesperides around the tree and, to the right, Herakles seated with his nephew Iolaos behind him. The mood of the scene, however, is not that of a life and death struggle for immortality, the idea behind Herakles' labour, but rather one of idyllic repose in a garden full of delights, the Elysian Fields attained, a spirit which invests most of the Meidias Painter's compositions.

The upper zone is much less frieze-like in design. The scene shows the Dioskouroi, Kastor and Polydeukes, come to steal the daughters of Leukippos. The two daughters of the king have been surprised, together with their companions, as they were gathering flowers in the sanctuary of Aphrodite. The goddess sits beside her altar at the bottom of the scene, invisible to all, while higher up is her stiff, archaic cult statue. To the left of the statue, Polydeukes has got his girl and is already speeding away in his chariot; to the right, and lower, Kastor is having more difficulty.

The composition, with its chariots pulling away from the centre and the fleeing women, is boldly centrifugal. In addition to the various ground levels in the Polygnotan manner are grasses, flowers and bay trees representing the groves of Aphrodite. The richness of the scene is further increased by the use of gilding on the cult statue and for necklaces and arm-bands, as well as the amazingly decorative quality of the painter's drawing. In the manner of the great wall-painter Parrhasios, who was said to have achieved the impression of volume through line, without the use of shadow, the Meidias Painter has used line to suggest volume, the fine folds of garments enveloping and modelling the forms beneath. All is rippling, transparent drapery, coyly tilted heads covered in fluffy curls, soft fleshy limbs and extravagant gestures: technique has perhaps supplanted taste.

The last decades of the fifth century in Athens also saw further experiments with matt colours on white-ground lekythoi, a typically Athenian shape and decoration almost never found outside Attica. By the last quarter of the century matt red and black were being used for the contours of figures and other objects, while an increased palette of additional fugitive colours, including green, blue and mauve, was developed for drapery and other areas of colour. On a simple but well-preserved lekythos by the Reed Painter, a work of the last decade of the fifth century, we find matt-black contours and a brilliant green (fig. 77, left). A youth and a woman stand before a tomb: the woman decks it with woollen fillets; the youth leans on his stick. The gesture of his right hand seems to link him with the woman tending the tomb, but a comparison with similar scenes suggests that he might be the deceased. There appears, at times, to be a deliberate ambiguity in the iconography of some of these lekythoi, an ambiguity intended perhaps to suggest the ephemeral nature of life on earth and the ever-recurring presence of death.

From the same workshop as the Reed Painter come a number of rather finer lekythoi, the 'Group R' lekythoi (fig. 77, right). On one of these a disconsolate woman is seen seated on the step of a tomb, her arms folded. Contours are here represented by short, broken lines which seem to suggest volume rather than accurately mark out its limits, again recalling the Parrhasian method that did not employ shading. The technique of shading (the ancient Greek term is *skiagraphia*) is associated with two other leading free-painters of the late fifth century, Apollodoros and Zeuxis. Shading can be found on vases for minor objects like shields, jugs or hats as early as the beginning of the fifth century, but it is not until its close that we see it used to create the impression of volume in human figures (male only). This occurs on a small group of huge lekythoi that are probably all the work of one artist. Their scale suggests that they were intended as substitutes for the marble lekythoi, which had now become popular as grave-markers.

The British Museum's Group R lekythos, however, seems to reflect interest in another technical device, namely perspective. One literary source attributes the invention of organized perspective (*skenographia*) to Agatharchos, a contemporary of the other free-painters just mentioned, who is said to have written a treatise on a stage-set that he painted for the performance of a play by Aeschylus, probably after the poet's death. In fact, partial linear perspective (foreshortening) was applied in

77 (a) *Lekythos showing a woman and a youth at a tomb. Made in Athens, 410–400 BC; attributed to the Reed Painter. Ht 31.8 cm. BM Cat. Vases D 73*

(b) *Lekythos showing a woman seated at a tomb. Made in Athens, 410–400 BC; attributed to Group R. Ht 51 cm. BM Cat. Vases D 71*

vase-paintings to both figures and objects from the end of the sixth century BC, but around the end of the fifth century there seems to have been a quickening of interest in such things on vases. On the Museum's lekythos the bottoms of the vases placed on the top surface of the large tomb are obscured as a result of the low viewpoint chosen for this partial perspective. This sort of low viewpoint is typical of the late fifth century, and it is only in the fourth that it was occasionally combined with a high viewpoint. As a result, we cannot be sure that Agatharchos' treatise sought to consolidate these two angles of vision into a single horizontal plane, which would have been the real beginning of a unified system of perspective. Nevertheless, we should conclude that such questions and attempts at answers were in the air.

We may close the fifth century, however, with a less experimental piece, a bell-krater the interest of which lies in the signature of Nikias, son of Hermokles, citizen of the deme Anaphlystos, in white around the foot (fig. 78). The scene shows a victory in the torch-race, a relay competition that formed part of the athletic events at several Athenian festivals. In the centre, the leader of the winning team holds his torch over an altar, while a winged Nike is about to tie a victory fillet around his arm. The torch-race was organized by tribe and the inscription on the headband of the victor's elaborate headgear clearly reads *Antioch...* (for the tribe Antiochis). The fact that the potter signs as a member of the deme Anaphlystos, which belonged to the tribe Antiochis, suggests very strongly that Nikias produced this vase specially for the celebrations following a victory by his own tribe.

As we have seen in this and the last chapter, some potters and painters may have been slaves, some foreigners and some citizens. The pottery itself gives the impression that in the sixth century the Athenian Kerameikos was made up of small family-based workshops. There was considerable expansion at the end of the century and this continued, with little detectable diminution following the destruction of the city by the Persians, until we can observe large *ergasteria* (workshops), such as that originally founded by Euphronios, employing so many painters that two even shared the decoration of one small cup. In the second half of the fifth century changes occurred: there are fewer signatures of potters and painters and there were perhaps fewer workshops active, but the craftsmen seem to have been particularly mobile.

At the beginning of this book it was noted that the archaeological evidence suggests that potters' workshops produced a wide range of

78 Bell-krater with a
victory ceremony for the
torch race; from Athens.
Made in Athens, 420–410
BC; signed by Nikias, the
son of Hermokles, of the
deme Anaphlystos, as
potter, and attributed to
the Nikias Painter. Ht
37.5 cm. GR 1898.7–16.6

material in addition to figured pottery. Although there is no room to
discuss here kitchen wares and lamps, the production of plain, black
slipped ware, which was at its peak in the second half of the fifth century, does deserve comment. Such vessels are to be found earlier than
the sixth century, but it is only from about the second quarter that the
Athenian production with its brilliant potting and wonderful, shiny
black slip came into its own and was in turn imitated in many other
centres of the Greek world (fig. 79). On a number of Boeotian black-
glaze kantharoi and skyphoi of the end of the sixth century BC we find
the proud signature of Teisias, who adds the fact that he is Athenian and
we may, therefore, be able to identify him as the Teisias whose name
appears on a fragment of a Little Master cup. This reveals once again the

79 Clockwise from left *Various non-Attic black-glaze vessels:*

(a) *Euboean kantharos; from Euboea.* GR 1882.7–29.12

(b) *Laconian amphora; from Kamiros (Rhodes).* GR 1864.10–7.258

(c) *Elean lekythos; from Galaxidi.* BM Cat. Vases G 89 *(GR 1893.7–28.4)*

(d) *Boeotian mug; from Boeotia.* GR 1931.2–16.14

(e) *Corinthian skyphos.* GR 1984.6–11.1

actual movement of potters, while also suggesting that the fact of Athenian production could be significant to the potential purchaser.

From shortly before the middle of the fifth century some black-glazed pottery began to be given incised or stamped decoration before the application of the slip. This idea seems first to have occurred in workshops that also produced red-figure pottery, thereby closely linking the two strands together. Stamped decoration was also imitated in other schools, for instance at Corinth, whither at least one Athenian potter seems to have gone late in the fifth century taking his stamps with him, in Elis (northwestern Peloponnese; fig. 79 c) and, of course, in Italy. Various types of ribbing were also produced, both vertical and horizontal, in the case of the latter often in deliberate imitation of Achaemenid Persian metal vessels. An example of one of the finest of the Athenian decorated products is a mug that employs not just ornamental stamps (maeander and ovolo) but also figural stamps to create the scene of the decapitation of the Gorgon Medusa by Perseus, aided and protected by Hermes and Athena (fig. 80). From the neck of the Gorgon spring both the winged horse Pegasos and the child Chrysaor. This Perseus mug is from Capua in central Italy and shows that Athenian black-glazed vases were as widely exported as their red-figure counterparts.

80 *Black-glaze mug with stamped designs showing Perseus killing the Gorgon; from Capua. Made in Athens, 440–430 BC. Ht 9.6 cm. BM Cat. Vases G 90*

8 THE FOURTH CENTURY BC

ITALY AND ATHENS

In 404 BC the long struggle between Athens and Sparta came to an end. Although capitulation came after much suffering, Athens' recovery was remarkably rapid and in a decade she was fighting Sparta again. In the 370s and 360s it was the turn of Boeotian Thebes to exert her power, especially under her vigorous leader Epaminondas, as the bickering between Sparta and Athens continued. Thereafter, mainland Greek eyes turned northwards, as Philip of Macedon rose to power. Further afield, in Sicily after the repulse of the Athenian expedition against Syracuse, the main threat came from the Carthaginians, but this was to be held at bay by Dionysios I, tyrant of Syracuse. After his death, there followed a period of instability and Greek Sicily degenerated into a fragmented shambles. In 344 BC an appeal was made to Corinth, Syracuse's mother city, and the aged Timoleon was sent, a man who with talent and even more luck, 'overthrew the tyrants, subdued the barbarians [Carthaginians], repopulated the greatest of the devastated cities, and then gave back the people of Sicily their laws', as his funeral decree relates. In Megale Hellas, the Greek cities of South Italy, it was Taras that came to the fore both politically and artistically.

In the world of the Kerameikos at Athens the rich style of the Meidian school had, by the second quarter of the fourth century, developed into what is sometimes called the Kerch Style. This name comes from the modern city in the Crimea that stands over ancient Pantikapaion, a Greek colony on the north coast of the Black Sea, where many fourth-century Athenian vases have been found. This export was most probably connected in some way with Athens' need to import large amounts of corn. In the Kerch style the sugary delicacy of the Meidias Painter's own works has, however, been replaced by a sketchier, harsher treatment with a great deal of added colour, especially white, yellow and gold. A rather finer than usual example is a bell-shaped krater found in Campania (fig. 81). It dates from around 370–360 BC and is the work of the Pourtalès Painter (named after the former owner of this piece). An elaborate multi-level scheme is used for this representation of the meeting of Herakles and the Dioskouroi to be

81 *Bell-krater depicting the initiation of Herakles and the Dioskouroi at Eleusis. Made in Athens, 370–360 BC; attributed to the Pourtalès Painter. Ht 51.6 cm. BM Cat. Vases F 68*

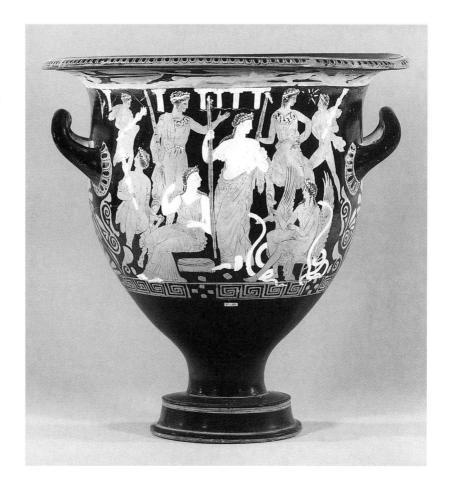

simultaneously initiated into the Mysteries of Demeter and Persephone at Eleusis. In the centre are Demeter, seated, and her daughter Persephone, standing, their flesh rendered in added white; on the right sits Triptolemos in his fabulous chair; and above stand two tall males who are probably the mythical ancestors of the two Eleusinian priest-hoods, Eumolpos and Keryx. The Dioskouroi approach from the upper corners, Herakles from the lower left. As prospective initiates they carry special rods of myrtle (*bakchoi*); the others hold torches, for it is night and the full moon shines up on the right of the columns which stand for the sanctuary of Eleusis itself.

The Kerch Style seems to have reached a peak shortly before the middle of the fourth century in the work of an artist known as the Marsyas Painter. On a splendid pelike (storage jar) from a woman's tomb on Rhodes we see Peleus come to carry off Thetis – a paradigm of ancient Greek marriage (fig. 82). There is much added colour in the manner of the Kerch Style – gold for Peleus' pointed hat and Thetis' hairband, and for parts of the wings of Eros, blue for the rest of his wings, and green for the drapery over Thetis' knees. Added white has been used to highlight both Eros and the naked body of Thetis.

The crouching, turning pose of Thetis recalls the later sculptures of Aphrodite bathing. This twisting action, which in nature and sculpture occupies space so well, can brilliantly evoke both depth and volume even in the two dimensions of painting. Thetis' legs are in profile, although the slightly higher left thigh helps to suggest depth, as does her stomach, but it is her breasts, one virtually in profile, the other nearly frontal, and her head turned round in three-quarter view toward her attacker, that really seem to pull the figure out into the third dimension. The fleeing sister up in the right-hand corner of the scene is of similar pattern, but the twist follows the other direction – near-profile legs, three-quarter buttocks, frontal back and, most remarkable of all, a *profil perdu*. This Nereid's elaborate pose, and that of Thetis, are probably derived from contemporary wall-painting, although elements of them are to be found much earlier – even the *profil perdu* occurs on a vase by Onesimos from the very beginning of the fifth century. Finally, the drapery continues the harsher style of the Eleusinian krater, in contrast to the clinging, almost wet folds of the Meidian vases. Here, however, the idea of pairing the fold-lines to hint at the darkness trapped between is used with greater confidence, with the result that the drapery of these monumental Nereids seems to recall the heavy satin gowns of some lavish costume drama.

The two schools in South Italy, the Apulian based on Taranto and the Lucanian centred on Metaponto, ran parallel for some years, but the Apulian school in due course expanded to new centres, whereas the Lucanian seems to have retreated into the hinterland in about 380 BC with the result that its products look more and more provincial.

In the Tarentine school there developed from the Sisyphus Painter's work two main streams of Apulian vases, the Plain Style and the Ornate Style. The latter was perhaps encouraged by the elaborate late fifth-century Athenian vases that were imported to places like Taranto and Ruvo. Around the end of the first quarter of the fourth century (c.380–370 BC) new elements were introduced to the Ornate Style, particularly in the decoration of the volute-krater. The artist who seems to have been responsible for these is known as the Iliupersis Painter (named after the depiction of the sack of Troy on one of his vases). His

82 Pelike showing Peleus and Thetis. Made in Athens, 360–350 BC; attributed to the Marsyas Painter. Ht 43.3 cm. BM Cat. Vases E 424

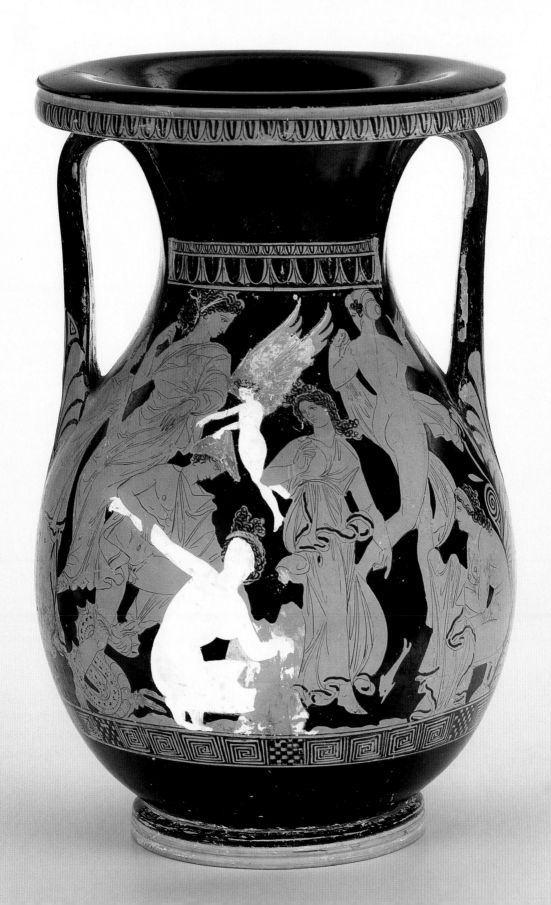

major innovation was the introduction of specifically funerary iconography to match the function of these monumental vases, which now seem to have been deliberately designed for the tomb. On a particularly elaborate volute-krater (fig. 83), we see a small temple-like structure (*naiskos*) with a youth inside – a representation of a contemporary grandiose Tarentine funerary monument. Round about are gathered youths and women who have brought offerings to the tomb. Added white has been used for most of the *naiskos*, for the youth and for the laver on which he leans, sorrowfully trailing his fingers in the water and thereby disturbing the reflection of his face; this added white must be intended to represent marble or stuccoed limestone. The upper part of the naiskos and the stool, on which the youth sits up on the right, are rendered in a sophisticated three-quarter view with a low angle of vision, an idea we have already seen on Athenian vases of the late fifth century. Here, however, the laver and the lowest step of the naiskos are also seen from a high viewpoint. This attempt to unify viewpoints may reflect Agatharchos' treatise, or developments on it. It is interesting to note that one of the other great free painters of the end of the fifth century, Zeuxis, was probably a citizen of Herakleia in southern Italy.

As a representative of the so-called Plain Style, we may take an interesting bell-krater with a comic scene, a vase attributed to the McDaniel Painter (fig. 84). At the centre an old actor with white hair and a crooked stick is being helped up the steps that lead onto the centre of the stage. He is labelled Cheiron, the wise old centaur who educated Achilles, and he is being pushed and pulled up the steps like a reluctant old pony – the crafty slave, named Xanthias, already on stage seems to be pulling him by his ears, while the old one pushing from below wears the mask typical of a cook. On the stage is Cheiron's large bundle, a yoke-shaped pole to help carry it over the shoulders and a bucket, no doubt laid down by Xanthias – all comic props that could let loose some ribald but well-tried gags, as another slave called Xanthias demonstrates at the beginning of Aristophanes' *Frogs*. To the right is a youth, perhaps Achilles or one of the other young heroes whom Cheiron educated. The two female actors that look on from behind a hillside are labelled Nymphai, perhaps those of the river Anigros where Cheiron bathed after being wounded by Herakles.

This is clearly a scene from a comedy about Cheiron. We know that Aristophanes' much older contemporary, Kratinos, wrote a *Cheirones* (Cheiron and his followers), while a number of fifth and fourth centu-

83 Volute-krater with visitors at a tomb. Made in Apulia, 380–370 BC; attributed to the Iliupersis Painter. Ht 68.8 cm. BM Cat. Vases F 283

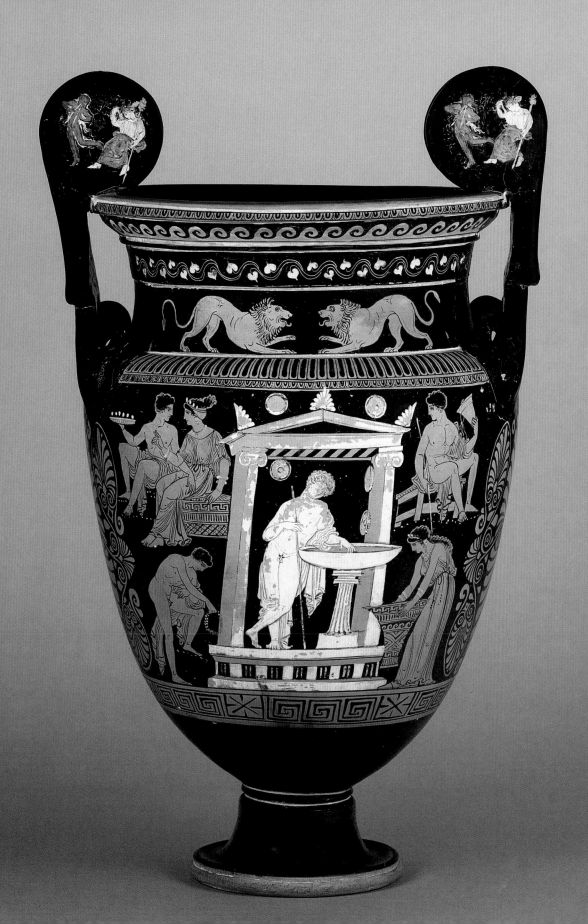

84 *Bell-krater with a comedy about the centaur Cheiron; from Apulia. Made in Apulia, 380–370 BC; attributed to the McDaniel Painter. Ht 37.4 cm. BM Cat. Vases F 151*

ry playwrights, such as Pherekrates and Kratinos the Younger, also wrote plays entitled *Cheiron*. It is difficult, therefore, to know whether such an illustration is taken from a contemporary work or the revival of an older work. It is clear, nevertheless, that drama, whether comic or tragic, was of vital cultural importance throughout Greece and the colonies, both west and east, and that Athenian plays were particularly popular.

It was in the second quarter of the fourth century that two new schools of South Italian vase-painters emerged further north, in Campania and in nearby Paestum. Dale Trendall, to whom we largely owe our detailed knowledge of South Italian vase-painting, suggested that the roots of these schools lie in the small group of artists active in Sicily (perhaps at Syracuse) in the last quarter of the fifth century, some of whom seem actually to have moved north to Campania and Paestum in about 370–360 BC. This migration may have been connected with the death of Dionysius I in 367 and the political disturbances that ensued.

An important tomb-group in the British Museum, the so-called Blacas Tomb discovered in the early nineteenth century by the Duc de Blacas at Nola in Campania, belongs to the very moment of this migra-

85 Clockwise from left *Vases from the Blacas Tomb at Nola:*

(a) *Skyphos showing a satyr and a maenad. Made in Campania, 380–370 BC; attributed to the Painter of Naples 2074. BM Cat. Vases F 130*

(b) *Hydria showing a Dionysiac revel. Made in Campania, 380–370 BC; attributed to the Revel Painter. BM Cat. Vases F 156*

(c) *Hydria showing Aphrodite and Peitho in a chariot drawn by Erotes. Made in Athens, about 390–380 BC; attributed to the Painter of London F 90. Ht 38.9 cm. BM Cat. Vases F 90*

(d) *Skyphos showing two nymphs. Made in Campania, 380–370 BC; attributed to the Painter of Naples 2074. BM Cat. Vases F 129*

(e) *Cup with Dionysos and Ariadne on the interior. Made in Athens, 390–380 BC; attributed to the Meleager Painter. BM Cat. Vases E 129*

tion (fig. 85). The two large skyphoi, which show satyrs, maenads and nymphs in rocky settings, are by one hand, the Painter of Naples 2074, who may have begun his career in Sicily. One of the hydriai, that showing a Dionysiac revel, is the name-piece of the Revel Painter, one of the earliest painters probably to be actually trained in Campania.

The two remaining vases from this tomb, however, are slightly earlier imports from Athens and may have been the prized possessions of the deceased, to which local vases were added on his death in order to make a set. The stemless cup with Dionysos, Ariadne and an Eros on the interior is by the Meleager Painter, an important artist who carried on the tradition of the Polygnotan group of vase-painters at Athens alongside the richer Meidian school. Gone, however, is the Polygnotan solemnity and under Meidian influence we find instead a certain sensuous ecstasy. The remaining hydria is by an imitator of the Meleager Painter, and shows a youth, perhaps Adonis, and a female charioteer in a car drawn by Erotes. More Erotes, satyrs and maenads escort the group, as Aphrodite sits and watches all – an all too florid flight of fancy.

In southern Italy the middle of the fourth century saw the Apulian Ornate Style reach its peak. One of the finest pieces of all is a large calyx-shaped krater, the name-piece of the Laodameia Painter (fig. 86). There are two friezes: the lower frieze has an extract from the fight between the Lapiths and the centaurs at the wedding feast of Peirithoos and Laodameia (our ancient sources give the name of the bride variously as Hippodameia and Deidameia), with both the bridegroom and his friend Theseus present. The upper frieze shows a woman sitting, head bowed and hands grasping her knees in agitation, while another woman langourously adjusts her hair, as a maidservant wields a white fan. The old nurse on the far left and the old shepherd near the right are both stock characters from tragedy, suggesting that the whole may have been taken from an otherwise unknown play, perhaps even Euripides' *Peirithoos*. The painting is exceptionally fine and one might at first think of influence from the Kerch vases of Athens: the eloquent poses and the use of added colours would not be beyond their painters' reach. The use of white dots to highlight the corners of eyes, however, and the attempts at shading and perspective from both above and below, neither of which occur on Kerch vases, suggest an increase in contact with free painting. If the best of the Kerch vases were to echo something of the work of the wall-painter and sculptor Euphranor, then the Laodameia Painter's work might reflect some of the innovations of Euphranor's successor, the wall-painter Nikias, who may have used such techniques as highlights more profusely than had been previously attempted.

Back in Athens, alongside the Kerch Style, there still existed the old black-figure technique, although it had been restricted, since the middle of the fifth century, to the Panathenaic prize-amphora. This vessel

86 Calyx-krater with two zones: upper zone, an enigmatic scene; lower, Perithoos and the centaurs. Made in Apulia, about 350 BC; attributed to the Laodameia Painter. Ht 76.5 cm. BM Cat. Vases F 272

87 *Panathenaic prize-amphora depicting Athena. Made in Athens, 367/6 BC; signed by Kittos as potter. Ht 71 cm. BM Cat. Vases B 604*

retained its traditional shape and decoration throughout the fifth centu-ry and was, indeed, sometimes painted by the leading red-figure artists of the day such as the Berlin Painter and the Achilles Painter. In the fourth century, too, leading painters such as the Pourtalès and Marsyas Painters produced Panathenaic prize-amphorai, but there were some innovations. Probably from early in the fourth century painters began to write the name of the *archon* (magistrate) for the year next to the right-hand column, and in about 360 BC the figure of Athena was turned to the right, instead of the left.

An exceptional piece, dating from about 367/6 BC bears the signature of Kittos as potter instead of the archon, who, to judge from the style, would have been Polyzelos (fig. 87). This signature, together with that of Bakchios on two other Panathenaics dating to 375/4 BC, helps us gain a precious insight into the world of fourth century potters. An inscription on a funerary monument from Athens and datable to about 330 BC, bears, in addition to the name of the deceased, Bakchios son of [A]mphis[tratos?] of the deme of Kerameis, an elegiac poem – 'Of those who blend earth, water, fire into one by skill, Bakchios was judged by all Hellas first for natural gifts; and in every contest appointed by the city he won the crown'. With this epitaph may be combined a decree from Ephesus dating to about 325-320 BC that awards citizenship of Ephesus to the Athenians Kittos and Bakchios, sons of Bakchios, and their descendants, since they undertook to provide 'the black pottery for the city, and the hydria for the goddess, at the price established by law', for as long as they remained in the city. Thus, we may surmise that the first Bakchios, who died in about 330 BC, had two sons, Kittos and Bakchios, who thereafter travelled to Ephesus, perhaps as a result of upheavals in Athens during the 320s. It is, however, extremely unlikely that the Kittos who made the London Panathenaic was the son of the first Bakchios, but he may well have been his brother.

This nexus of information not only provides evidence of family involvement in the production of pottery over two generations by Athenian citizens, but it also hints at competitions for some public contracts at Athens, most probably for the production of Panathenaic prize-amphorai (pieces with signatures and no games inscription, such as those of both Bakchios and Kittos, might well be samplers). There is also clear evidence of the actual placing of contracts for black-glaze pottery in Ephesus, especially hydriai for Artemis (presumably these were to be used for bringing the water from the spring near the temple). Since we do not know of any black-glaze hydriai that were actually made in the latter part of the fourth century at Ephesus (unless imported Athenian clay was being used), we can only presume that what Kittos and Bakchios did was to secure the export from Athens of batches of black glaze pottery, including hydriai, most probably from their own family's workshop back in Athens, still manned by their uncle Kittos and his children.

It is interesting to note, therefore, that there was indeed a substantial production of large, even monumental black-glaze vases of very high

88 Black-glazed hydria with gilded decoration in the form of a necklace; from Capua. Made in Athens, 340–300 BC. GR 1871.7–22.8

quality in the second half of the fourth century. These include kraters, hydriai (fig. 88), amphorai of Panathenaic shape and large pelikai, all with gilded relief decoration, especially in the form of necklaces or wreaths. They were highly prized in many parts of the Greek world, including the northern Black Sea, Rhodes and the East Greek cities, Egypt and Italy. It seems quite possible, even probable, that some of them are products of the Kittos/Bakchios workshop in Athens.

A perfectly preserved Panathenaic prize amphora bears the name of the archon Niketes, and so can be dated to 332/1 BC. The reverse shows

89 *Pankration: detail from the reverse of a Panathenaic prize-amphora. Made in Athens, 332/1 BC. Ht of panel 29 cm. BM Cat. Vases B 610*

a pankration, an all-in fight that knew only two rules – no biting and no eye-gouging (fig. 89). In the centre, one athlete has caught the other's head in a tight head-lock, while he pounds the back of his neck. The scene is framed by a vigilant trainer or umpire and the next unfortunate contestant. The use of gilding and added white on Athena's drapery and the frontal and three-quarter faces of the athletes are typical of fourth-century Panathenaics and echo preferences in red-figured painting.

Later fourth-century Athenian imports to Campania such as these might suggest their possible influence on local South Italian vase-painters. Indeed, the increased use of added white and additional colours in the third quarter of the century could bear witness to this, but there was also a good deal of influence from the flourishing school in Apulia, whence a number of painters seem to have actually migrated. At this period there seem to have been two major centres of production within Campania, one at Capua, the other at Cuma. A tall neck-amphora from the Capuan school may stand as an example (fig. 90, left): a woman is offering a warrior a drink on his departure; he wears a breastplate made up of three circles, and a plumed helmet. These accoutrements are typical of native Oscan warriors, and it is possible that such vases were produced especially for the local non-Greek market.

90 Opposite (a) *Neck-amphora showing the departure of a warrior; from Santa Agata dei Goti. Made in Campania, about 350–325 BC; attributed to the Libation Painter. Ht 54.2 cm. BM Cat. Vases F 197*

(b) *Hydria depicting two women at a tomb. Made on Sicily, about 320–310 BC; attributed to the Lipari Painter. Ht 33.4 cm. GR 1970.6–19.1*

91 Right *Bell-krater showing Alkmene on the pyre; from Santa Agata dei Goti. Made at Paestum, about 350–340 BC; signed by Python as painter. Ht 56 cm. BM Cat Vases F 149*

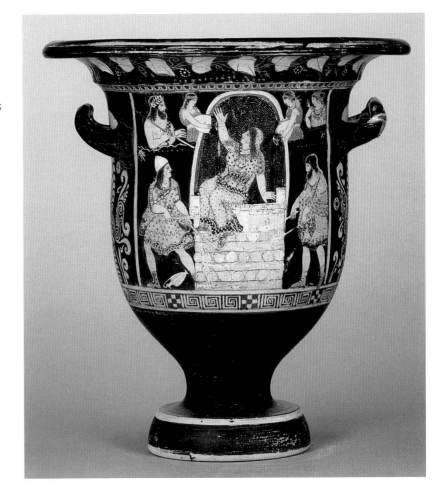

Around the middle of the century yet another local school had developed on the border between Campania and Lucania, centred on Paestum. The origin of this school seems to have been Sicilian, as was that of the Campanian school. There were two main painters in the Paestan school and, unlike all other South Italian potters and painters, they have actually left us their names, Assteas and his slightly younger companion Python. A splendid bell-shaped krater signed by Python gives us some idea of their style (fig. 91). The large, fleshy figures with their grand gestures have a very rich, almost operatic quality, while the treatment of the subject may well owe something to Euripides' play, *Alkmene*. Amphitryon suspected that his wife, Alkmene, might have been unfaithful to him with a rich lover (it had actually been Zeus) and threatened her with death. When she took refuge on an altar he followed her to burn her off the altar. Here we see Amphitryon, on the right, setting torches to a pyre of logs placed in front of the altar on which Alkmene sits, while on the left Antenor helps him. Alkmene raises an arm in supplication to Zeus, who is shown in the top left-hand corner and is balanced by Eos, goddess of the Dawn, on the upper right. Zeus has thrown his thunderbolt (shown in white next to the logs in front of Amphitryon) in an attempt to stop Amphitryon and this is followed by the Clouds, who pour water down from their jars to quench the flames. The remarkable rainbow effect around Alkmene is probably to be understood as part of the *ekkyklema*, a stage device which allowed a prepared tableau, in this case Alkmene on the pyre, to be wheeled out onto the stage.

92 Volute-krater with visitors at a tomb. Made in Apulia, about 325 BC; attributed to the Baltimore Painter. Ht 88.9 cm. BM Cat. Vases F 284

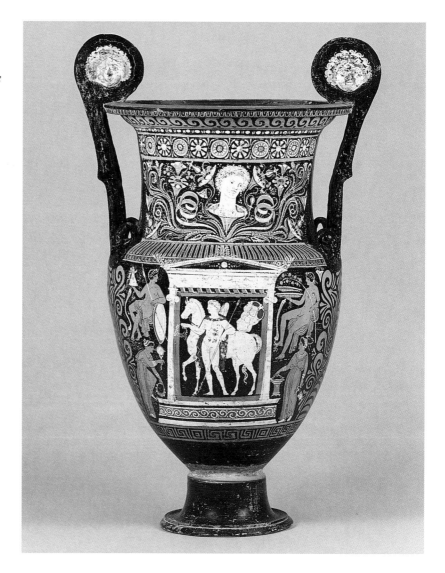

The third quarter of the fourth century also saw the final flowering of the Apulian Ornate Style and the amalgamation of the Plain Style into the Ornate. A large volute-handled krater by the Baltimore Painter, one of the most important Apulian painters of the last third of the century, exemplifies the full-blown late Ornate Style (fig. 92). A large funerary naiskos dominates the body of the vase, and within it are the statue of a youth and his horse, together with his breastplate. On the neck there is a female head in added white amid an elaborate spray of curling and twining flowers and tendrils. This idea, like the naiskos, goes back to the Iliupersis Painter and may be considered the hallmark of developed Apulian vases. It has been suggested, however, that it has its origins in the sphere of free painting, especially the work of the panel-painter Pausias who was active in the middle of the fourth century.

In Sicily there was something of a renaissance in pottery in the last third of the century. After the beginning of the second quarter of the century and the migration of some Sicilian potters to Campania, the production of vases seems to have continued, especially in the east of the island, but only in a rather limited fashion. It was only after about 340 BC, following Timoleon's expulsion of the Carthaginians when political stability returned, that there was a recovery in terms of volume and some Campanian artists may have quit their adopted home for that of their fathers. There is little Sicilian pottery outside Sicily, but the British Museum does have a hydria by the Lipari Painter (fig. 90, right), which dates from around 320 BC, showing two women at a stele (funerary marker). The maid merely holds a triangular fan, but the mistress reveals considerable emotion, raising one hand within her cloak up towards her mouth, as she holds a box of eggs, an offering for the dead. Vases by the Lipari Painter often display an extensive use of added colours, and on this piece a blue can still be seen on the women's long chitons below the hems of their cloaks. The front of a somewhat related skyphos in Palermo, from Falcone, is entirely in added colour and where the colour has flaked off one can make out what are probably abbreviations of the Greek words for the colours that were to be added on top: they include blue, red and yellow. Such vases were presumably the Sicilian equivalent of the Athenian white-ground lekythos, intended solely for funerary use.

There is perhaps little to admire in the South Italian vase-paintings of the end of the century, but one final group, the so-called Gnathian pottery, is refreshingly simple and unpretentious. This style developed shortly before the middle of the fourth century, perhaps in Apulia,

93 (a) *Gnathian bottle decorated with a swan set in a floral design; from Cyrenaica. Made in Apulia, about 330 BC; attributed to the Stockport Group. Ht 14 cm. BM Cat. Vases F 582*

(b) *West Slope cup-kantharos with floral decoration and the painted inscription, naming Dionysos. Made in Athens, 270–260 BC. Ht 9.7 cm. GR 1908.4–10.8*

where it was soon produced in great quantities, but the idea was also taken up by painters in Campania, Paestum and Sicily. The technique relied on the application of added colour, usually white, yellow and red, to a black-glaze vase. A simple bottle dating from around 330 BC from the Stockport Group gives us some idea of the freshness and charm that these vases can achieve (fig. 93, left): it shows a swan set in a floral spray that continues the tradition of Pausian florals found on the neck of the Baltimore Painter's volute-krater. The decoration here, however, is purely ornamental and, after a few early pieces, almost no attempt was ever made to take advantage of the full possibilities of the technique.

Gnathian pottery is the only South Italian fabric that seems to have been exported in any quantity and the swan bottle, found in Cyrenaica in North Africa, is among the earliest of such exports. During the rest of the fourth century and the early third, Gnathian vases are occasionally to be found in Egypt, on the Aegean islands, at Athens, on Cyprus and along the coast of the Black Sea. Indeed, it seems that the markets to which the Athenians had turned in the fourth century, as exports to southern Italy became more difficult owing to the rise of the local schools, began after the final collapse of Athenian vase-painting around 320 BC to accept Gnathian exports. The red-figured vases of southern Italy lasted a little longer, perhaps until about 300 BC; Gnathian, however, was still being produced during the first quarter of the third century.

9 THE HELLENISTIC PERIOD

The rise of Macedonia under Philip II reached a climax under his son, Alexander. His campaigns secured him an empire that stretched from Greece to Afghanistan. But, when Alexander the Great died in Babylon in 323 BC, there was no suitable heir and for the next forty years his leading generals and their sons fought a series of wars for various parts of that fast fragmenting empire. Three main Hellenistic dynasties were to emerge – the Ptolemies in Egypt, the Seleucids in Syria and the Antigonids in Macedonia – but in the third century a number of smaller kingdoms broke away, most notable of which were the Attalids of Pergamon. The late Hellenistic period saw Rome gradually eliminate each of these major dynasties. For Athens, the end came after she had joined cause with Mithradtes VI of Pontos against Rome, for this led to Sulla's destruction of the city on 1 March 86 BC.

Alexander's campaigns brought immense wealth in the form of booty and this perhaps contributed in due course to the rise of a well-to-do bourgeoisie, especially in the eastern Greek cities. The new centres of power resulted in new artistic directions and new systems of artistic interrelations. The beginning of the third century saw the end of the red-figure technique throughout the Greek world and with it essentially the end of the concentration on the depiction of the human figure, although the black-figure technique survived at Athens for the ritualized scenes on Panathenaic prize amphorai even down to the time of Sulla's sack.

One of the most important sequences of vases in the Hellenistic period is the so-called West Slope Ware, named after the material found on the western slope of the Acropolis at Athens. This owes its origins to the gilded black-glaze products of the later fourth century (cf. fig. 88). The chief difference is that instead of gilded relief the decoration was done with an added yellowish white and with incision. Some influence from the late Gnathian products of Apulia may have encouraged this simplification, but similar products are also to be found in Corinth. West Slope Ware was produced from the third century to the first in a number of centres around the Mediterranean, including Athens, Corinth, Macedonia, Crete, Cyrenaica, Egypt and Pergamon. On the right of fig.

94 (a) *West Slope jug bearing a Medusa head in relief on the neck, and three-dimensional cubes on the body; from Cyrenaica. Made on Crete in the early second century BC. Ht 28.3 cm. BM Cat. Vases G 12*

(b) *West Slope amphora. Probably made at Pergamon, second century BC. Ht 23 cm. GR 1994.7–28.1*

93 is an example from an Athenian workshop, a delicately potted drinking vessel of the second quarter of the third century. This kantharos has in addition to a floral chain, the word 'Dionysou' ('of Dionysos'), thus neatly linking decoration to function.

On Crete, at the end of the third century and the beginning of the second, we see some unusually elaborate West Slope vases. One series consists of bowls with the head of Medusa moulded in relief in the centre and bright polychrome patterns around. The British Museum has a companion piece, a hydria-shaped jug with a Medusa head applied to the neck (fig. 94, left). This head is surrounded by a very vivid, three-dimensional pattern built up of triangles of white, yellow and simple reserved clay, bounded by incised lines, and all intended to represent Athena's scaly aegis in which Medusa's head was set. The same combination of incision and added colour occurs in the patterns on the shoulder and the body. The perspective cubes on the body are particularly

three-dimensional, but such a tectonic pattern might seem hardly suitable decoration for a simple pottery vessel.

Next to the Cretan jug stands an amphora with necklace and wave pattern, as well as vertical ribbing on the lower body (fig. 94, right). This was probably made in Athens under strong influence from the new centre of Pergamon, which had begun to play a prominent role under its Attalid rulers from shortly before the middle of the second century.

In addition to this light-on-dark technique, there were a number of dark-on-light fabrics. Some, such as those of Canosa in Apulia and Centuripae on Sicily, the former of the third century, the latter of the second, are overly florid in both plastic additions and painted decoration, which was regularly done after firing, thus rendering them closer to terracottas than pottery. Crete, however, seems to have been the home of one of the more restrained wares, the so-called Hadra vases, named after one of the cemeteries of Alexandria in Egypt where they were first identified. Hadra hydriai, the finest of which employ a black-figure technique, have also been found on Crete and elsewhere around the Mediterranean, but it was only in Egypt that they were used as inscribed ash-urns. These inscriptions, some incised as on fig. 95 ('of Dorotheos'), others written in ink, nearly always refer to the funerary function of the vases and normally consist of the name of the deceased (male or female) whose ashes the vase contained. The most elaborate give not only the deceased's lineage, home and rank, but also the precise date of death and an indication of the reason for his or her presence in Egypt, usually an embassy.

Another dark-on-light fabric is represented by a series of squat jugs (*lagynoi*) and pyxides. Many of these were produced in a centre somewhere in the area of Pergamon, although there was another prolific centre on Cyprus and some were even made in Egypt itself. Over a thick white slip a brownish paint has been used to depict floral garlands and various objects connected with feasts – fig. 96 shows a nice conceit, a silhouette representation of a lagynos. Our ancient literary sources describe the shape of the lagynos, adding that it made a gurgling sound as wine was poured from it, and reveal that symposiasts took their own lagynos full of wine to a feast.

The most commercially successful Hellenistic ware, however, was the so-called 'Megarian Bowl' (fig. 97, right). This type of mould-made deep bowl with relief decoration was produced in many centres throughout the Hellenistic world – in Athens, Corinth, the Peloponnese, the islands

95 *Hadra hydria used as a funerary urn for Dorotheos. Made on Crete, about 200 BC; attributed to the Dromeus Painter. Ht 35 cm (foot missing). GR 1995.10–3.1*

96 *Squat jug (lagynos) of the Lagynos Group, decorated with garlands and a lagynos; from Benghazi. Made in the area of Pergamon, second century* BC. *Ht 15.9 cm. BM Cat. Vases F 513*

97 Below (a) *Silver floral bowl with gilded details; from Bulgaria. Greek, third century* BC. *Diam. 15 cm. GR 1989.7–24.1*

(b) *Mould-made Megarian bowl with floral decoration. Made in an East Greek centre, about 100* BC. *Diam. 13.7 cm. GR 1865.7–20.29*

98 (a) *Pergamene red relief ware kantharos with relief decoration and incision; from Laodicea. Made in the area of Pergamon, about 50 BC. Ht 16 cm. BM Cat Vases L 35*

(b) *Cyrenaican red ware amphoriskos with added white decoration; from Benghazi. Made in Cyrenaica, early first century BC. Ht 10 cm. GR 1867.5–12.50*

and the Greek cities on the coast of Asia Minor, as well as in Italy – from the third century BC to the first. Such bowls seem to have been made first at Athens and were perhaps inspired by silver bowls actually brought over from Egypt in connection with the foundation of the Ptolemaia, an athletic festival instituted in honour of Ptolemy III Euergetes in the mid 220s BC. The decoration is often floral in character, but there are also many with figured scenes. The technique of production involved centring a mould on the wheel and then throwing the vase inside it. An extended lip was sometimes then thrown on. A comparison between a silver bowl of the first half of the second century and an East Greek pottery imitation of the end of the second century BC points up the relationship (fig. 97, left). There are the same broad leaves (*nymphaea nelumbo*) rising from a bed of fern-like acanthus leaves – note the way that both *nelumbo* and acanthus bend over towards the viewer.

Some late West Slope Ware of the early first century BC reveals the deliberate use of a red slip instead of a black one – accidental red had become more and more common from the middle of the second century (cf. fig. 97, right). An example is a local product of Cyrenaica, a delicate neck-amphora with a debased ivy chain on the shoulder and a garland chain on the neck, all in added white and without incision (fig. 98, right). At Pergamon, the red slip has been decorated with moulded relief elements – here they are floral but on other examples they are figural – and feathery incised scrolls (fig. 98, left). When a deliberate red slip is set alongside the use of a mould we might think that we are across the boundary into Roman pottery and the beginnings of the late first century BC pottery known to us as Arretine Ware. It is, however, important to realize that there was no such boundary, not even really a series of separate boundaries in different parts of the Mediterranean, for ever since the middle of the second century BC Rome sought to exert her power beyond Italy – and the Greeks never stopped being Greek. Nevertheless, with the beginning of the mass production of Roman fine ware and its export all over Europe we come to the end of our survey of more than six thousand years of pottery produced in Greece and the Greek world.

10 CONCLUSION

THE POTTER AND HIS CLIENTS

This book began with the technology employed by a Greek potter; we may end it by considering his clientele. In Archaic and Classical Athens, an important customer was the city-state, the *polis*, for it was the city that let the contracts for Panathenaic prize-amphorai (figs 42, 87 and 89) and for sets of black-glaze vessels that were used in the *syssitia* or public dining places instituted by the democracy. Pottery for burials, however, was presumably often bought in a hurry by surviving relatives to be placed in the tomb on the third day after death, so that there was rarely the chance to plan such purchases, although there were clearly exceptions (cf. fig. 61, the Brygos Tomb). Some pieces were specially ordered for a variety of occasions. An example for private use is the remarkable Corinthian aryballos that has a portrait of Aineta ('I am Aineta') with nine admirers listed in two columns below (fig. 99). An interesting example of a piece specially ordered for dedication in a sanctuary is a fragment of a Chiot kantharos from Naukratis, the Greek trading post on the Nile Delta, which was specially ordered by a woman named Aiguptis, no doubt one of the *hetairai* (call-girls) for which Naukratis was famous, to be dedicated in the temple of Aphrodite (fig. 52 d) – and this order was presumably placed through an intermediary.

In Athens potential private purchasers had two options. One was to stroll up the streets leading out of the city to the northwest through the Kerameikos and view the material being made in the *ergasteria* (workshops), rather as one can still do today at Amaroussi in northeastern Athens. The other method was to go to the Agora in the centre of Athens and see what was for sale at the *skenai* (stalls). These two options are exactly those that the poet of the *Kiln* mentions when he asks on behalf of the potters that their pots 'may receive the price due to their value, many being sold in the market, and many in the streets'. The customer who wished to make a special order, specifying a scene or shape or wanting a personal message, would have gone to the *ergasterion* of his choice. For a quick retail purchase the answer was presumably the *skenai*, although it is quite possible that some of these stalls were actually staffed by a particular potter's family rather than an independent retail trader.

The sheer quantity of Greek pottery that was exported, the existence of pieces ordered by distant customers and the imitations of forms produced at the end of the trading route, all suggest that potters may well have developed arrangements with particular traders or shippers, who not only took the pottery to Italy or Egypt, but also came back with recommendations as to what might do well or even with precise orders. On a number of Athenian vases from Italy, indeed, we find cryptic marks or letters scratched under the feet that most probably distinguish the shipper – in one or two cases the name is written out in full. One series of marks that take the form of the two letters *SO* has been plausibly linked with a trader from Aigina called Sostratos, who is even mentioned in Herodotos as having achieved great wealth. Sostratos' activity in the latter part of the sixth century in Italy is revealed by part of a stone anchor dedicated by him to Aeginetan Apollo at the port of Etruscan Tarquinia. The appearance of the *SO* mark under a neck-amphora potted by Nikosthenes (fig. 48 c) of a form specially developed for the Etruscan market perhaps demonstrates a special commercial relationship in operation. It is also possible that members of some potters' families themselves became directly involved in such long-distance trade.

99 Early Corinthian aryballos with a portrait of Aineta on the handle plate and her admirers listed below. Made in Corinth, 620–600 BC. Ht 6.6 cm. GR 1865.12–13.1

Pottery was, of course, made of simple fired clay and did not, therefore, require a large monetary investment in terms of raw material, but it did require considerable hard work, great skill and time. The prices that Athenian vases fetched in the Agora or abroad are hard to estimate from the very few examples of inscriptions under bases that mention money, for we do not know whether such amounts refer to sale in Athens, sale at the end of a trade route or even a second-hand value. Such prices as survive range from a $^1/2$ obol to 18 obols (6 obols = 1 drachma). But let us take one example: under the foot of a hydria very like the one in fig. 66 is inscribed *hy 2 drach poi* ('hydria 2 drachmai painted'). At the time of the production of the hydria the Athenian state paid its jurors a 'subsistence rate' of 2 obols a day, while a mason or a sailor might earn a drachma a day. Thus, in our terms, we might guess that the hydria might have cost something between £50 and £100.

Material value and purchase price, however, were not the only measures of value in ancient Greece. The many examples of ancient repairs, the existence of a second-hand market (most clearly in the case of Panathenaic prize-amphorai), and the frequent use of pottery as a gift both for the gods and for the dead all indicate the esteem in which pottery was held. Furthermore, alongside Kritias' celebration of pottery and the potter's wheel as Athens' greatest contribution to mankind, one might also bear in mind Plato's value-judgement: 'If a skilful potter had made the vessel smooth and rounded and well-fired, like some of the fine two-handled jars that hold six choai, if he should ask us about such a vessel as this, we should be obliged to agree that it was beautiful.' That pottery brought wealth to its producers, as well as its traders, is demonstrated by the dedications of potters on the Athenian Acropolis, such as those of Mnesiades and Andokides, and of Euphronios. However, the social status of such potters and painters who were not slaves or *metoikoi* (foreign residents) most probably varied with the prevailing social conditions. For example, their status may have been extremely low during times of aristocratic rule or even bourgeois domination, but at moments of transition, for example at the end of the tyranny and during the first decades of democracy, they may have enjoyed greater freedoms and privileges. It is interesting to note, therefore, that at just such a moment, the last decade of the sixth century and the first two of the fifth, Athenian potters and painters seem to have been at their most exuberant, self-promoting and wealthy.

FURTHER READING IN ENGLISH

J.D. Beazley, *The Development of Attic Black-Figure* (posthumously rev. edn, Los Angeles, 1986)

J. Boardman, *Athenian Black Figure Vases* (London, 1974)

J. Boardman, *Athenian Red Figure Vases: the Archaic Period* (London, 1975)

J. Boardman, *Athenian Red Figure Vases: the Classical Period* (London, 1989)

J. Boardman, *Early Greek Vase Painting: 11th–6th centuries BC* (London, 1998)

J.N. Coldstream, *Geometric Greece* (London, 1977)

R.M. Cook, *Greek Painted Pottery* (3rd edn, London, 1997)

V.R.d'A. Desborough, *The Greek Dark Ages* (London, 1972)

O.T.P. Dickinson, *The Aegean Bronze Age* (Cambridge, 1994)

I. Freestone and D. Gaimster (eds), *Pottery in the Making: World Ceramic Traditions* (London, 1997)

J.W. Hayes, *Handbook of Mediterranean Roman Pottery* (London, 1997)

S. Hood, *The Arts in Prehistoric Greece* (Harmondsworth, 1978)

D.C. Kurtz (ed.), *Greek Vases: Lectures by J.D. Beazley* (Oxford, 1989)

J.V. Noble, *The Techniques of Painted Attic Pottery* (2nd edn, London, 1988)

G.A. Papathanassopoulos (ed.), *Neolithic Culture in Greece* (Athens, 1996)

T. Rasmussen and N. Spivey (eds), *Looking at Greek Vases* (Cambridge, 1991)

M. Robertson, *A Shorter History of Greek Art* (Cambridge, 1981)

M. Robertson, *The art of vase-painting in classical Athens* (Cambridge, 1992)

B.A. Sparkes, *Greek Pottery: An Introduction* (Manchester, 1991)

B.A. Sparkes, *The Red and the Black: Studies in Greek Pottery* (London, 1996)

A.D. Trendall, *Red Figure Vases of South Italy and Sicily* (London, 1989)

INDEX